Tello J. D'Apery

Europe Seen through a Boy's Eyes

Tello J. D'Apery

Europe Seen through a Boy's Eyes

ISBN/EAN: 9783337211912

Printed in Europe, USA, Canada, Australia, Japan

Cover: Foto ©Andreas Hilbeck / pixelio.de

More available books at **www.hansebooks.com**

Europe Seen Through a Boy's Eyes.

BY

TELLO J. d'APERY.

WITH TWENTY-SIX FULL-PAGE ILLUSTRATIONS.

New York:
Published by the Author.

THIS LITTLE BOOK IS DEDICATED

TO

MY FATHER AND MY MOTHER.

TELLO J. d'APERY.

PREFACE.

I would not write a preface if I was sure that my book was good enough to go forth without some excuse. My youth must plead for me where I have not done all I ought. My trip was a hurried one, and all I could do was to try and show you how one portion of Europe looked, seen through a boy's eyes. I now send forth this, my first book, hoping that it may escape the notice of the critics, and fall into the hands of my most indulgent friends.

THE AUTHOR.

CONTENTS.

	PAGE
CHAPTER I. ACROSS THE OCEAN. GIBRALTAR	9
CHAPTER II. TANGIERS	21
CHAPTER III. GRENADA	41
CHAPTER IV. SEVILLE	57
CHAPTER V. MADRID	66
CHAPTER VI. A BULL-FIGHT IN MADRID	74
CHAPTER VII. BURGOS TO THE RIVIERA	84
CHAPTER VIII. GENOA	96
CHAPTER IX. PISA	104
CHAPTER X. FLORENCE	113
CHAPTER XI. NAPLES	131
CHAPTER XII. VESUVIUS	156
CHAPTER XIII. NAPLES AND CAPRI	172
CHAPTER XIV. ROME	185

CHAPTER I.

ACROSS THE OCEAN. GIBRALTAR.

IT was the fourth of March and about the hour when President Cleveland was being inaugurated that the *Kaiser Wilhelm* was just outside Sandy Hook, rising and falling on the high waves. The lamp in the lighthouse showed fitfully, as the big steamer rose or fell. It was blowing a terrible gale, and snow and sleet were driving before it, and ice covered the decks. It was almost impossible to see anything, or at least I found it so, as I stood on the deck in a quiet corner struggling with three emotions till then unknown to me. I was leaving my father and mother and making my first flight out into the great world alone. I was leaving my country, and my little paper which has been so much to me during the past four years, and I was beginning to feel that peculiar sensation that is the advance guard of sea-sickness. Altogether my emotions overpowered me so that with tears or sleet or perhaps both, my eyes were blinded and I sought the seclusion that the cabin granted, like the captain of the good ship *Pinafore*.

After that retirement there followed a short period of misery that I will not mention. The first thing I recollect clearly was the antics of my steamer trunk. That was small, but packed as full as it could hold and it was heavy. Down in one corner were three pounds of Huyler's best, all done up in pretty boxes, and a number of other little things that boys like. These were packed by the loving hands of a dear friend who died while I was away, to my great grief and sorrow.

That trunk had sharp corners bound with iron, and when the ship would roll one way it would slide downward to bang against the partition, and then rebound and slide back again and slam up against the side of the ship with a vicious thud, and then slip back to the partition only to return and hit the side with another corner, just as if it was determined to dig a hole through before morning. Every time it flew backward or forward it seemed to get new momentum and I lay there and feebly counted the times it hit and wondered exactly how long it would take that sharpest corner backed by about a hundred pounds weight to batter a hole in the ship, and I remember that I felt unable to put out a hand to stop it or to find voice to ask some one else to, and I was quite sure that I should have been incapable of trying to save myself even if it did make a hole big enough to let the whole Atlantic in.

Then I fell asleep and when I awoke the steamer was going as steady as a clock, and there was no more storm, and I was soon on deck. Words cannot express what I felt when I was sea-sick, every time I would think of that candy, and I firmly decided that I would write a strong editorial that should make all boys as willing as I to give up the pernicious habit of eating candy, yet four days later we all thought candy never tasted so good and the editorial did not get written.

Life on shipboard, I suppose, is the same to all who go across the great sea. We played shuffleboard, checkers and chess, we listened to the band, promenaded, and read books, and wondered when we should reach Gibraltar. We counted the runs and bothered the captain and everyone else with questions, changed our American loose money for foreign coins, and I decided to buy a dog and a mandolin. Any further plans were cut short by seeing a ship in distress. This ship did not signal for aid, and was on her way, probably, to the Azores, but she looked as if she had been beaten nearly to pieces on sharp rocks, and her masts and sails were also in a sad condition.

We had several passengers on board who knew all the conundrums that have ever been written or made, and as we had no possible manner of escape we had to stay there and listen, and pretend we enjoyed it; but, I think that was one of the reasons why we were so delighted when we saw the great Rock of Gibraltar rising from the horizon. We passed the Azores and thought them very picturesque and pleasant, and very fertile. The steamer passed right through them and we could see numbers of windmills, and the people could be seen walking about. Fayal is, I think, the prettiest of the group. All of them look like extinct volcanos.

After passing the Azores we soon sighted the shores of Portugal, and saw the most of that coast in outline, sometimes distant and sometimes near, and we reached Gibraltar just about dark. We had expected to pass by Gibraltar and leave the steamer at Genoa, and go from there to Florence, taking all the other places we visited, in line, as we came back, but as cholera had been reported at Marseilles it was decided to change our itinerary and "do" Spain first, as Spain was about to declare a quarantine against Marseilles.

The great rock grew bigger and higher and looked grimmer and more towering as we approached it, and it seemed fairly above us as the steamer came to anchor. It looked like a giant guarding the Gate of Hercules, and keeping perpetual watch for foes.

When we approached, our baggage was brought on deck, and we said a few good-bys to those who remained on board, and thanked the officers for the care and kindness we had received and as soon as the steamer anchored we tumbled and scrambled into the little boat that landed us at the foot of the Rock of Gibraltar.

When we neared the landing we turned and looked at the *Kaiser Wilhelm* as she lay rocking idly on the tide, for it had been a second home for us so long that we all felt a pang of regret, but, as soon as we found that we were on solid land again new things and thoughts claimed our attention. I stamped hard to feel the ground, and remembered Sancho Panza's words: "Oh, happy cabbage planters of Seville. They have one foot in their cabbage garden and the other not far away." Solid ground is more to my taste than sailing over water where the bottom is from three to six miles deep, and nothing to catch on to.

The instant we landed we were surrounded by hotel guides and custom house officers, all talking at once, and in a language strange to us, until we were nearly distracted. Finally the guides drew back a little, and after the custom house officers satisfied themselves that we had no liquor or cigars, we were permitted to pass through the gate.

We went slowly up to the hotel, leaving our trunks until morning. Our first night on shore was restless and uneasy, and I was glad when daylight came. I was out at half-past five watching the English soldiers drill. The whole place seemed to be under arms, and English soldiers were everywhere, filling the streets and crowding the Spaniards, Jews, and Moors to the walls. Look where you will, an English redcoat always formed the foreground of the picture.

GIBRALTAR.

I strolled around delighted with the clean fresh look of everything, and presently came to where a Moor was sitting outside of his little store, enjoying the first rays of the rising sun, and he answered me in fairly good English when I addressed him, and he seemed delighted to talk with an American as I certainly was to have a chance to talk with a real live Moor on his own ground. He finally directed me to where I wished to go and we parted sadly, I because he had no Moorish money, and he because I did not buy anything else he had.

Afterward I reached the dock, where I made a search for our trunks which I found with difficulty, as there were two or three Spaniards perched on each, and evidently they had been there all night, hoping thus to secure a claim for a franc or so for bringing them up to the hotel. As soon as I came near they began to quarrel as to who had the best right to carry them, and as the dispute bid fair to last all day, I beckoned to a fat fellow, who fairly walked all over the others, to reach me, and then I struggled for ten minutes to make him understand the name of the hotel, and finally had to go with him myself.

After breakfast we took a cab and went for a drive to that beautiful place they call Europa Point. On each side tropical trees and plants lined the way, giving it a doubly pleasant look to persons just arrived from a land covered with ice and snow. We left the carriage and went up higher to get a better view. Below us was the beautiful smooth Mediterranean, behind, the green valleys and mountains of Spain, and beyond lay the Atlantic blue and broad, and to the south we could see the hilly coast of Africa like a lovely picture. I cannot find words to tell how beautiful it all seemed, and the clear blue sky and fresh air lent it all a new charm.

On returning we visited the galleries that have been mined out of the solid rock, and looked at the wonderful works that had made of this mountain the strongest fortress in the world. One soldier told us that they had ammunition and food enough to last for seven years of siege.

People are not allowed to go up to the signal station, but we went up and into the part that is honey-combed with passages and holes in which monstrous guns are mounted. We walked out on a little ledge from which we got a fine view of the town and the pretty bay. We could see the soldiers marching on the shore, like little specks, and we were often startled by flocks of birds that flew around. As we slowly descended we caught glimpses of the shores of Africa with its old Moorish towers set on the hills. Every turn in the road gave a new outline to the hills across the straits, and I think it was then that we all decided to go to Tangiers that looked so enticing across the water.

I do not know how high Gibraltar is nor how many cubic feet of stone there are in it. I know that it is a grand sight seen from its base, and a most beautiful one seen from its summit.

GATE OF TANGIERS.

CHAPTER II.

TANGIERS.

THE next day was one of great excitement. We left early in the morning for Tangiers in a small steamer. The weather which had been fair and mild took a sudden turn and became stormy, and the passage though short was very rough, but nothing happened until the steamer came to anchor, and we had to get into the small boat to be rowed to the land by the Moors. The steamer anchored not far from two fair sized steamers which formed the Sultan's entire navy.

We should have reached the shore all right if the rowers had not left off work to argue about how much they were to charge for our trunks. When they stopped rowing the boat swung around broadside to the waves, and a huge one struck the boat and dashed over it. There was a gentleman and his wife in the boat with our party, and both ladies were drenched. Charles and I sprang for the shelter of our trunks and escaped, but all the rest were wet through, and I was afraid that Aunt Mary would get a chill, but the Moors grasped their oars and turned in the heavy sea, and at last brought us to land, with no more deluges.

We landed and walked briskly up to the gate, where a custom house officer sat smoking, and he nodded gravely as we passed him but did not appear to feel equal to speaking. We were told that we must wait until our guides got donkeys for us to ride, and we stepped into a sort of vestibule to wait, and to shelter the ladies from the wind but we were quickly ordered out again by signs, and we found that we had entered a mosque where no Christian was ever allowed.

We bore the waiting as best we could until the donkeys came, but they got there at last, and we managed to get the ladies mounted with some difficulty, on account of their wet clothes, which hung heavy and from which still trickled little streams of water.

Tangiers is picturesque as you see it from a distance, and it is beautiful then. It is picturesque after you get in it, but it is not very enticing. We rode along the shore passing long caravans going and coming from the desert, and we entered the gate and rode through the narrow streets as rapidly as was possible on account of Aunt Mary and the other lady. The hills are steep and the streets run right over them up and down and sidewise, and the poor beasts of burden toil up and down to the constant music of sticks rattled over their bones, and the cry of *Aura,* which means to go on. I saw no carriages or other vehicles in Tangiers except a cart for garbage.

As soon as we reached the hotel we took the wet dresses to the kitchen to dry and the ladies went to bed to get warm and rest after their rough experience. I went to the kitchen and coaxed the fat cook to give me some peculiar looking but very good cakes. Then Charles and I left the ladies to rest and went out for a donkey ride.

We went up to the Market Place and found that we had just happened to hit upon a market day, and the open space was covered with people, perhaps a thousand of them — men, women and children, of all shades of color and none white. Some of them were Arabs and some Moors, and the others I do not know the names of, and they were dressed in the loose, flowing robes and

TANGIERS.

burnouses, and some wore turbans on their heads, and some wore the Turkish fez. The women were all covered with veils, some white and some dirty. I cannot tell what a strange look all this had. There was a telegraph pole here and there, and some of the houses had a European look, but all the rest seemed to be thousands of years old and millions of years distant from our civilization. The dress of the people was so different from ours, their looks and manners, too, that it seemed as though it could not be in the same world with us and only a few hours distant from the triumphs of civilization.

Donkeys were everywhere and there were a good many horses, too, there, some of them pretty miserable and some of them truly splendid creatures. But a horse with a New York dude "rising to the trot" in Central Park, and a Bedouin Arab on a horse are two things. It is a pleasure to watch an Arab ride. You cannot see him move his hand or foot, and yet the horse will turn, run, gallop, walk or stop, so that it is wonderful. There is no jouncing or riding up and down, the horse and the rider have one head, one body and one mind that controls all. It is fine.

I think Market Day is once a week, and the natives come in from outlying hamlets and each brings what he has — a little lime, a little charcoal, or some trifling thing, and some had some of the dirtiest looking candy you ever saw. I used to think hat some that the Italians in New York offer for sale was bad enough but this is far beyond theirs.

Charles and I succeeded in getting donkeys, and as we rode through this crowd of people we were assailed on all sides for money, by some of the most wretched looking people I ever saw, nearly all of them blind. I was told afterwards that nearly all the blind men were thieves who had been deprived of their sight as a punishment; though what they could find to steal in this forsaken country I cannot imagine.

We rode along until we came to a place where there was a snake charmer performing his tricks, and we halted to watch him. There was a ring of people gathered around him and as we approached I saw that he was cut in many places. Our guide said that was to keep the poison of the bites from entering into his system.

He opened a goatskin bag and let out his snakes. They were not the sleepy kind you see in the circus but lively and vicious, but he chanted and beat on his drum until they seemed to become tame. I cannot tell all the horrible things he did with the snakes, but at last after letting one bite his tongue, he threw the snake down and grabbed a handful of grass and began blowing for all he was worth and soon little jets of smoke began to come, and then a little flame came out of his mouth. I do not see how he did it, but it was wonderful. He did several other curious tricks, but we did not stay until the end.

Near by was another ring of people and in the centre there was a story teller, and he told his stories whatever they were with a good deal of spirit and acted them all out. The people listened attentively, but seeing that they were told in their language they did not interest us much, and we left there headed by our guide.

We passed through the principal streets, through crowds of people who hardly moved enough to let us pass, and such poverty I never saw. Every one, almost, was in rags, and always looking for a stray coin, and every hand was held out in appeal.

We kept on under old arches and through narrow alleys and between queer-looking dwellings, objects of as great curiosity to the people as they were to us. We came to a mosque where there was a long row of shoes before the door, belonging to the faithful who were inside saying their prayers. The worshippers take off their shoes on entering the sacred place, but Christians are not allowed in the mosque on any pretext.

The next place of interest that we saw was the prison. It does not seem possible that such things can be in this century. The prison is a miserable place, and there is a hole in the wall which permits you to look in and the unhappy creatures inside to look out. In that small place were twenty or thirty people, all huddled together, ragged, thin, hungry, and altogether in a terrible condition. As soon as the prisoners saw us they held up their bony hands begging for something to eat, or money to buy it with. One man held up a pale and sickly looking baby and asked for something for it to eat. We gave him something, and the tears rolled down his face. I do not see why this poor little baby is kept in this foul prison.

We visited the bank and what a bank! There was nothing in it but some empty boxes. The doors were nothing but iron bars, with four large padlocks that were ready to fall to pieces. A guard sat outside and when we had transacted our business he followed us more than a block, talking and gesticulating wildly because we did not give him more. Our guide said he always did that and not to mind him, and as we did not understand what he said it did not hurt us, and we paid no attention.

We returned to the hotel without accident, but after some excitement caused by the wicked old donkey that Charles rode. He insisted on stopping to reflect every few minutes and it took some time and a good deal of labor to get him started again. He seemed to be as Charles expressed it, "all dried up" and he needed oiling.

The ladies had got rested and dried and went to visit a Moorish harem. We went along and had the exciting pleasure of sitting outside and waiting till they finished their visit. Aunt Mary told us afterward about the harem — that it was quiet and clean, with matting on the floor and some sort of divans but nothing remarkable. The women, three of them, I think, were dark and appeared very much pleased to receive the visit. One fell in love with Aunt Mary's earrings and wanted to trade with her for some pinchbeck jewelry of theirs. I believe they did exchange some little presents.

That evening after dinner we went to a Moorish cafe, where huddled up in a little room were several musicians playing on a lot of stringed instruments. Seated around were all the noblemen of Tangiers, smoking, and playing cards for money. The tobacco that they smoke has, they say, Indian hemp in it, and it stupefies the smoker. The musicians play and sing and smoke until they are so overcome that they dance around like children. One of the musicians offered me his pipe, but I declined with thanks, and he seemed glad that I refused for he smiled and kept on smoking until he began to get gay and clap his hands and sing; and such singing as it was! The music had all gone from his voice, and it was a serious matter to sit and listen and make no sign of the agony I was enduring.

We had a talk with the richest man in Tangiers, and found out that his fortune was about five thousand dollars of our money. He intended then to come to America and have a Moorish cafe at Chicago, but I did not find him there. This man tol us that

STREET SCENE IN TANGIERS.

a person could live luxuriously in Tangiers on two hundred dollars a year.

We were glad to leave the close atmosphere and get out into the open air again. Aunt Mary fell in love with a lantern that the guide carried, and was going to buy it; but it was too big to carry, so she had to leave it. The streets have scarcely any lights, and every one who goes out at night has to carry a lantern, which would be a fine signal for a robber hidden behind a dark corner.

Next morning early Charles and I took a ride around town, and he couldn't get any other donkey than the poor dried up one that had made us so much trouble the day before. We rode out of town to see as much of the surrounding country as we could. The scenery is not as fine as it looks from Gibraltar, and the vegetation is rather scanty, with a good many prickly-looking plants. But on the whole there was a fair amount of cultivation. Orange and lemon groves were numerous, and sugar cane, olives and other things are to be seen on every side; but the farms, if they can be called that, are all small, and have poor houses and no good stables.

There were several quite rough ravines, and the guide, who was on foot and who found no difficulty in going as fast as our animals, led us over several very steep places along the banks, where, if the donkeys had slipped we would have had quite a fall and a nice ducking; but I believe that donkeys never do fall.

A snake glided out from a bunch of weeds and disappeared on the other side of the road in the thick grass; the guide said there were many kinds of very venomous serpents there.

We entered an orange grove and the guards were picking oranges. The fruit looked so tempting that we yielded and ate several. The trees were literally breaking under the weight of fruit and presented a beautiful sight, with the golden balls and green foliage, and under them the lovely carpet of long grass and scarlet poppies.

When we had finished we mounted again and on going towards the gate found a fountain, where a number of Moors were washing their feet. Why they chose such a conspicuous place for the purpose I do not know. Several of them turned to the shady places and in a few moments, while we looked at the men at their ablutions, picked and brought us a bunch of sweet violets, and they presented them to us with closed mouths and ready hands. Of course we understood and gave them some small coins for their pretty thought.

We then proceeded on our journey around the town, or rather city, for Tangiers has a population of about 18,000. The roads are very poor, and lined with all sorts of rubbish, besides the Moors and their trains of donkeys. As we approached the city we turned and looked backward. There was the early morning sun shining on the caravans that were just coming over the distant hills, and here and there a mounted soldier standing so that both he and his horse were outlined against the sky. There were hundreds of Moors going to the market place, and we followed, passing along by the walls where there was a caravan encamped. It was an interesting sight.

There was a gray, weather-stained tent, with a savage-looking Arab sitting at its door. There were camels and donkeys, some of them loaded with bundles of grass twice as large as themselves. There were one or two baby camels with funny little faces, and seeming to be all legs and feet.

EARLY MORNING SCENE IN TANGIERS.

There were Bedouins in their queer-shaped hoods and mantles, and all these were clustered around the tent—all quiet and waiting for some word of command to wake it up.

Just inside the gates there was a sort of rude bazar where I think they made a commerce of old and new burnouses. On the walls were dozens of them hanging like so many codfish, waiting a customer. Women with covered heads and bare feet moved around like ghosts, and strange looking men in turbans, or red fez, or pointed hoods moved to and fro with dignity. On the ground there sat several merchants, each with all his stock in a little basket. I never saw anyone make a sale while I was in Tangiers, excepting when one of our party bought something.

We entered the place by the North gate and rode toward the centre of all attraction, the market place, where the crowd was as great as the day before. Our guide kept up with the donkeys and even persuaded them to go faster, and this I consider remarkable, for he was on foot and the road rough and stony.

We saw Selim, our general guide, who was with Aunt Mary who had gotten out for the first time since the disaster to her dress. She and our other friends had been looking all over for us, and it was almost impossible to get through the crowd, but at last we met, and started on over the same ground we had travelled the day before, and we all found many things of interest, not so much on account of its excellence as from the Oriental flavor over it all. I bought a curious dagger for a paper knife for a dollar, and a red fez with a white turban to go around it, and I put it on to the intense amusement of the people, for no one but priests or married men wear the white turban. I found it comfortable, so I didn't care. The rest of our party bought little souvenirs of one kind and another and I decided that if I did buy a puppy I would call it Selim.

After this promenade we returned to the hotel and had lunch and started back to Gibraltar. The passage was very rough and nobody felt very well. Altogether it was the most uncomfortable voyage I ever took. The spray came over the boat and wet us, and the poor steerage passengers were not in it at all. They were about the most miserable set I ever did see. I wonder why it is that the poor have to take all the miseries, and suffer so.

As we skirted along the coast of Africa, our attention was called to the numerous watch towers half a mile apart, where the Moors used to send alarms all along the coast in times of danger, by lighting bonfires on the tops of the towers.

Tangiers from a distance began to grow beautiful again, nestled up along the side of the hill and extending almost to the edge of the sea. The buildings showed out whitely against the blue sky and green trees, and the strange architecture grew more and more fascinating as we drew farther away, yet the passage was so rough and unpleasant that we were all glad to see the big rock of Gibraltar towering above our heads, and we were soon at the hotel and happy to be there.

ARABS ENCAMPED OUTSIDE THE WALLS OF TANGIERS.

CHAPTER III.

GRENADA.

AFTER a good night's rest we took the boat for Algerciras, a small town across the bay from Gibraltar, and there I had my first experience on a European railroad train. After having been examined by the custom house officers for anything contraband we took a lumbering old stage to the station, where we were to commence our tour through Spain. We found our train waiting for us, and it looked more like a lot of horse cars hitched together and drawn by a prehistoric monster, than a train of cars as we have them. The cars are about half as long as our American cars and divided off into compartments which hold from six to eight persons.

When the train pulls out of the station the conductor — who, I think, must be the missing link between man and monkey, he was so agile and climbed along the outside platform so well, hanging on by his side-whiskers half the time — locked us in, and no matter what happened we couldn't get out until we reached a station.

You get in with any- or everybody that goes first class. The second class is much worse than the first, and the third class is terrible, or at least I thought so as I peeped in when I was on the platform. When the cars start they jerk and struggle and fly back and do all sorts of things, but at last go off at a slow, uneven pace.

There was not a good chance to see the country as the windows are small, and those who sit in the middle of the stuffy seats can not look out. We reached Grenada that evening, tired and dusty but so glad to get out of the car that we did not feel cross.

Grenada is so beautiful that no words could describe it, and it is no wonder that so many persons go to see it. The scenery is quiet and peaceful, and the Sierra Nevada Mountains in the distance and the blue rivers, the Darro, the Genil, and the Vega, winding along at their feet made a lovely background. The city is large and quaint and picturesque, with many interesting things to see.

We rode along in the hotel coach and were more than delighted with what we saw. Aunt Mary looked at the neat little balconies plastered up against the houses like swallows' nests, and where there sat beautiful Spanish ladies dressed in bright colors, with rich black lace mantles over their heads, and wanted to transport one, ladies and all, and fasten it on her own house.

These little balconies are often carved and highly ornamented, and have hangings of tapestries thrown over them. It was all so different from anything I had seen that I grew quite enthusiastic. Down in the streets it is quiet, much more so than any place I had yet seen. There were sleepy-looking men lounging up against the walls, and ladies sitting silent in the balconies. Even the children were not very noisy except one party where they were playing at bull-fight. One big boy was on his knees, for the bull, and three others were hopping around him with sticks for lances and old rags for the red cloth.

The streets are not very wide nor are they very narrow, but the houses are so different from ours on the outside that as I looked at the carvings, and noted the massive styles and strange architecture I could think I was dreaming. Donkeys were everywhere. They lined the roads and patiently bore all sorts of burdens, from grass which they were not allowed to nibble, to as many people as could crowd on them. I noticed one sleepy little fellow with a white nose, whose master was half lying on top of half a ton or less of grass, which covered the donkey all but his nose, and the man was playing on his guitar while the poor little beast plodded on. The donkeys provide free music in Spain for all who like it.

Our hotel was at the end of one of the most beautiful drives I ever saw, and there we passed two most delightful days. We had a fine dinner that night, and I rose early the next morning and was looking about to admire the country and to see all I could, when I came across some of the servants in a little enclosure milking goats and donkeys. After that I was afraid to eat or drink anything in Spain. I left that scene and walked on up a hill where I got a fine view of the whole great valley, and the dim mountain peaks beyond. Long, winding roads stretch off in every direction, through the hills and valley, and little streams come tumbling down from the hills and go off to meet the river in the distance. I could see on the summit of a hill the buildings of the famous Alhambra, which have for so many centuries been the admiration of all who love beauty, but I overcame my desire to go up there then, as we were all to go up after breakfast.

As we approached the door of Justice, which is the entrance to the Alhambra, the guide began his speech about a gloved hand over the first arch, but his English was so bad that we could not understand what it was all about, but it was very impressive and we all listened gravely.

From the outside the Alhambra does not give any idea of the wonders of its interior, but it looks like a great cluster of massive buildings of different shapes and sizes. It is only when you get inside that you can understand it. Every room or gallery leads to and is a part of something else, and the fineness of work and richness of color is so great that it is a long time before it can be taken in detail.

We went up the narrow passage which leads to the watch tower, where Cardinal Mendoza first hoisted the Christian flag. The Alhambra was built by the Moors and was begun in 1248 and finished in 1354. The whole edifice covers an oblong square 770 yards long by 200 wide and is on a spur of the mountain range of the Sierra Nevada Mountains. There was a strong wall all around it flanked by thirteen towers. It is said that there is space between the walls and the Alhambra to allow 40,000 soldiers to camp. All this has trees and shrubs and in many places fountains and other ornamentation, but it is not well kept up. There was a little village with a convent and other quite large buildings erected within the walls, but this seems to be pretty nearly in ruins now. I think the Alhambra should be left alone in its solitary grandeur, but care be taken to maintain it in good preservation.

The Alhambra has been the dwelling-place of kings from the Moors to Christian monarchs for many centuries, and it is worthy of a royal owner. The name "Alhambra" means the red house. The palace of the Moorish kings consists of a group of buildings of red bricks. On one side of the square of the tower is the unfinished palace of Charles V.

The two principal courts are the Court of the Lions and the Patio del Eslanque; the

COURT OF LIONS, ALHAMBRA.

Court of Lions is one hundred feet long and fifty wide, surrounded by a colonnade ten feet deep, formed of Moorish arches and columns.

The floor of the court is paved with beautifully colored tiles, and everywhere is the inscription in blue enamel and gold, in Arabic, "There is no conqueror but God." In the centre there is a fountain supported by twelve lions, which look as much like lions as a friend of mine of the same name does. They are very mild and gentle looking lions. Perhaps they have been tamed by the elements and the passage of time. It is curious that men capable of working out the wonders of this wonderful palace could not have carved out better looking animals, but their talent seemed to all run to the intricate work on the buildings.

The basin of the fountain is of Oriental alabaster. The other principal court is the

Patio del Eslanque, and has a large fountain filled with fishes, in the middle, with marble steps on each side which lead to the bottom. I think this must have been for a bathing tank.

The decorations are all of stucco and mosaic and vary in color, which is wonderfully preserved. On one side is a circular room, with its elegant cupola, and its beautiful designs in stucco on the walls. It is said that Abu Abdallah assembled his Abencerrages in that room and cut all their heads off and let them fall into the fountain, and the guides show some red spots on the marble as proof.

Opposite this hall is a little one which connects with the apartments of Charles V. and thence to the Sultana's dressing room. In one of the corners are tiles which were perforated, and the guide told us this had been done to let perfumes rise from the rooms below.

The Whispering Chamber, the Hall of the Ambassadors and the Audience Hall are a few more of the wonderful rooms to be seen in this marvel of architecture. Rooms open out of rooms, and galleries out of galleries till I believe one might be completely lost in the Alhambra without a guide.

The Hall of the Ambassadors occupies nearly, if not quite, all of the Comares Tower, and the light enters through windows and doorways. The latter lead out into gardens, but from there you can look out on the plain of Grenada. The stucco ornaments are nearly two feet deep, and seen from a short distance look like jewelry. The tiles and mosaic work in this room are very small compared with some of the others, but the coloring is wonderful, much of it having more yellow than any other color. There is in this great place the remains of a platform where it is supposed the throne was placed. It would take months of study to know all the beauties of the Alhambra.

It is said that there are mysterious underground passages arranged so that people could escape in case of danger, but those we did not see.

One of the saddest sights is the palace left unfinished by Charles V. The rest had been built and occupied, and had had, so to speak, their day; but this beautiful palace fell into ruins before it was ever inhabited, and the empty window casements stare out in a most melancholy manner.

One of the most beautiful effects is that of the bright sun shining down through the unroofed courts. The sky is so blue above, and the shadows and sunbeams playing among the columns and arches are so clear cut that the more one looks at it the more beautiful it is.

There is scarcely any marble used in this vast place. It is nearly all stone and brick, and tiles set into the stucco in the most fantastic shapes and designs. That is, if they are taken singly; if taken altogether it has a wonderful beauty and smoothness. The mosaics are made of colored tiles, not of broken stones as they are in some other places seen later. These are richer in coloring than the stone mosaic work, and far handsomer.

We were at the Hotel Washington Irving, named so, I think, to attract American tourists; but, it was said there that it was in consequence of his beautiful description of the Alhambra.

Grenada is beautiful always, but I think it is most so at early morning or just at sunset. There are nightingales in the woods, and they sing once in a while, and when they are not singing you can sit and feast your eyes on the beautiful landscape and wait for them to begin again.

A lady of our party was sure that she heard one close to the hotel, but, we discovered that it was a poor hen that was being sacrificed for our luncheon on the train, and I must say that aside from the chicken the Spanish hotel keepers are not to be recommended for putting up lunches. Ours was mostly basket, with sour bread and eggs, more remarkable for strength than anything else. One was so very strong that it was with difficulty that I got it out of the car window, and they have curious ideas of dressing a chicken.

As I said before, there are many donkeys in Grenada, also beggars, many of them gypsies. On our return from the Alhambra, we met the king of the gypsies. He struck a kingly attitude and let us admire him, then offered to sell us his photographs for

GYPSY KING IN GRENADA.

forty cents apiece. As soon as we had bought one he bowed and returned to his royal dignity backed by a stone wall. He carried a long staff and was dressed in the old Spanish style. His people lived at a little distance from the city, and I was told that the most of them lived in caverns hollowed out of the mountain side. It is said that it is very interesting to go and see their dances, particularly at their festivals and weddings, but it was not the right time for that while we were there.

Charles and I took a short gallop through the little villages surrounding Grenada, on horseback, but as it threatened to rain we were obliged to return. The horses we saw in Spain were not very handsome, and though the Spaniards ride well they manage their horses more through the pain of the cruel bit they use, than by gentleness such as is shown by the Arabs of

Tangiers. It was pleasure to see them ride, and quite the reverse to see the Spaniards on horseback.

That evening we started for Seville.

CHAPTER IV.

SEVILLE.

WE were in Seville, and found it a beautiful place with even more of interest than we had found in Grenada. It looked more alive and fresher and newer some way. The people, too, I fancied looked more alert, and the houses had for the most part a more modern appearance, yet it was all so different from our own country that it had all the delight of a strange sight. As we wandered through the city we could see beautiful gardens, through the lattice work of the gates. These were wrought very finely, in a great variety of patterns of iron, and some were gilded. There were *patios* inside with fountains and no end of flowers of every kind. I suppose it was not very polite to peep through these gratings at the private gardens inside, but we did it, and often saw statues and splendid carvings around the fountains. After all, it may be that these open gratings were put there on purpose for people to look through.

After a long stroll through the city, we went to the Alcazar, which the guide tells you was built for a palace for Don Pedro the cruel. The palace is beautiful in its design and coloring, and has an Oriental look. The color and patterns are woven in together so that they look like cloth like that they make the India shawls of. The roofs of the different portions of the immense building rise in domes of different sizes, and the effect is very light and graceful, and it reminds one very much of the Alhambra, but is in better

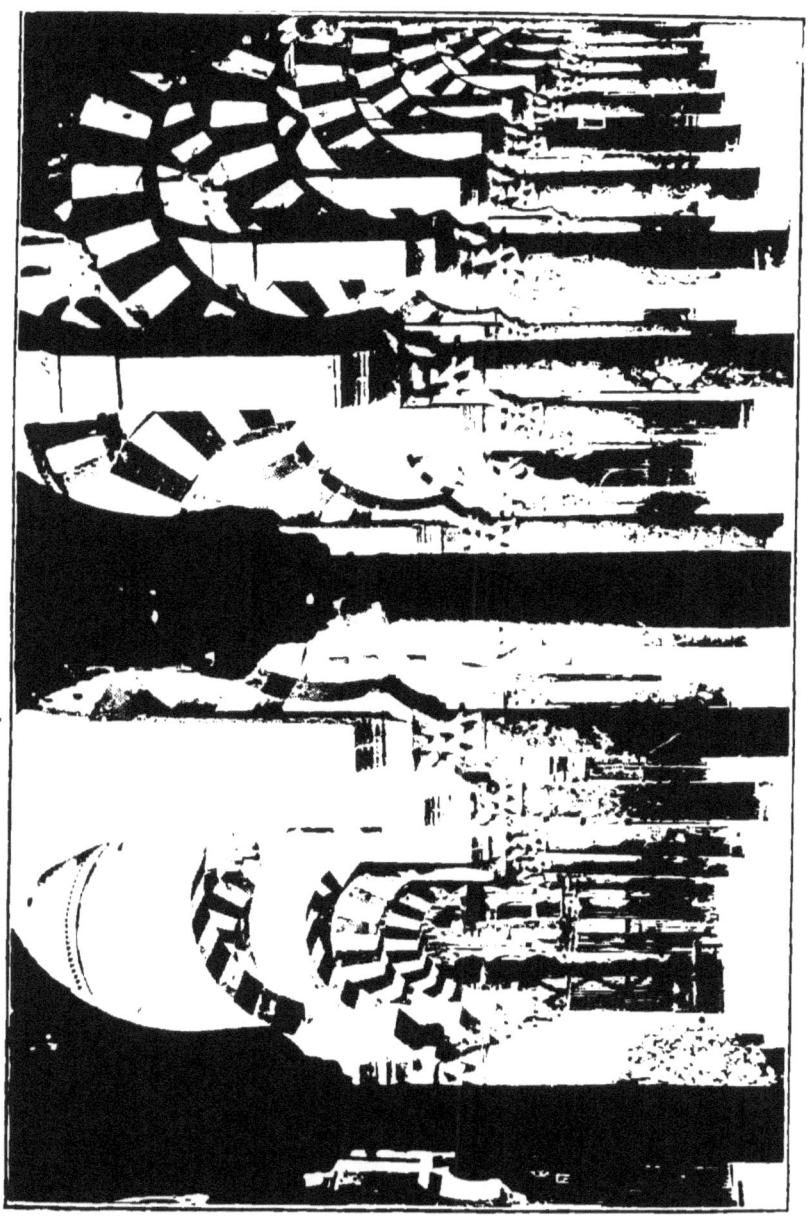

CATHEDRAL IN SEVILLE, FORMERLY A MOSQUE.

preservation. The colors on the walls in the mysterious patterns are as fresh as if they were painted yesterday.

After we had gone through the Alcazar and admired all its beauties to the full content of the guide, we visited the Cathedral, which is a fine building, and the Giralda stands by its side. The Giralda is a tower and was built by the Moors, and seeing what beautiful work they did, and noting that nearly all the fine buildings in Spain were built by those same old Moors, I think it is a pity they were driven away.

The Giralda is the lightest and most graceful tower I saw abroad. It is said that the tower at Madison Square is modelled after it, but as nearly as I can recollect ours cannot be as large. We went to see the picture gallery where there are twenty-four pictures by Murillo, and we also saw his house.

It is a pretty sight to watch the people come out of the Cathedral. The ladies nearly all wear the Spanish mantilla. When they wear it to church the lace falls over the hair down to the forehead, and at other times it is put on the head over the high comb and a couple of red roses, and then carried backward and crossed over, and is held by only one pin. The ends are brought around across the waist and fastened there by some more roses. If ladies knew how pretty they would look in these lace mantillas every woman in America would want one. I bought one for my mother.

The children in Seville are dark, but pretty, with large, dark eyes and white teeth, and they are always laughing. The ladies are pretty, too, and the men are polite and never too busy to speak kindly to a stranger. I liked Seville very much. We went to the market place and bought a number of trinkets which are very cheap, and several kinds of fruit. The oranges are delicious.

After this we saw some of Columbus' work, and some of his writing, and a number of other curiosities, and then we went to a tobacco factory where seven thousand women were employed, three thousand of them in one room. Those who had babies took them along with them when they went to work, and they were taken care of. It is said that it makes the people very sick with cramps when they first begin to work in a tobacco factory, but no one that I saw looked sick. The little children were all rosy and plump and as lively as tadpoles in a pond.

We went to see the House of Pilate, which a rich man built after he had been to the Holy Land. He had this house built as an exact reproduction of Pontius Pilate's house in Jerusalem. Everything looked so strange and different from the things outside the building that one could well believe it was in some far off country and that we were living in the time when such things were.

Seville is a walled city, and is built on the banks of the Guadalquiver. The walls are over three miles around and for the most part are in a good state of preservation. It is a beautiful city, seen from both outside and inside. It is mostly built of light-colored building material or painted in bright colors, that is, the wooden portion is. This city, with its Alcazar, and all its greatest edifices was originally founded by the Moors. On the hills surrounding Seville are numbers of ruined castles and towers, and everywhere are orange and olive gardens. The Alcazar is nearly as fine as the Alhambra.

Several of the churches were originally mosques, or Moorish towers, rebuilt or altered enough to serve the purpose, and over it all there hangs a mysterious air of the dead and gone past.

We would have liked to stay in Seville longer, but our time was limited, and that evening we left for Cordova and reached there the next morning and we had but a short time for sight seeing. We drove through the principal streets, and to the grand mosque, which is another place built by the Moors, and as it was too beautiful to destroy, and besides would have been a good deal of work, it has remained to be a centre of interest. Cordova is a very old town, and the houses are weather-beaten and ancient. There are many very ancient families who live in Cordova, in their old feudal style, as well as it can be made to fit in with nineteenth century ways. They drive out every fair evening in open carriages, it is said, and go slowly through the quiet streets to the regular promenade, and they bow to their friends, and listen to the music of the band as their carriages pass and repass the music stand. Then they drive over the old bridge and back home.

This city is walled, and the wall was built, the guide told us, by the Romans who founded the city, and seen from outside looks much like an old fortress, and it has a more ancient appearance than the other cities in Spain, more I think in the shape and outlines of the wall and buildings than any actual decay.

The bridge was built by the Romans and all through the city are remains of their style of architecture, and there are arches, temples and gates still in pretty good preservation. We all like to look at ruins and relics while abroad, but I don't believe Americans would care very much to have them home. The great Cathedral was built for a mosque, and that mosque was built on the spot where the Romans had had a temple to Janus.

This Cathedral looks like a fortress outside and is enormously large on the inside, giving the idea of immense space. There were rows on rows of beautiful columns of semi-precious stones. I think there are over a thousand columns.

All the country around seems to be very fertile, and certainly it is beautiful.

CHAPTER V.

MADRID.

AFTER we had seen all that we could crowd into one day we left Cordova for Madrid and reached there the next day, having passed Toledo without stopping. We stayed in Madrid four days.

I cannot begin to tell half of the things I saw in Madrid. There was so much to see, that it is confused, and, if it had not been for more sedate-minded Charles I should not have been able to place anything, as he kindly furnished me his notes of what we saw there.

Madrid is a grand city but not well placed, as it is in the middle of a wide plain, when it could have been built on some of the low mountains that surround it. The streets must have originally been goat tracks, as the oldest parts of "old Madrid" are the most crooked I ever saw, and I have been to Boston. But the more modern portion has straighter streets, some broad and fine. The public gardens look from a distance like a colored patchwork quilt. The Prado is one of the finest drives in the world. Everywhere there are statues and trophies and historical houses, and the homes of the old nobility of Spain. Each of these families has a history that is generally associated with the history of the country in some way.

As to pictures Madrid is rich in the choicest works of most of the Old Masters, and I think I saw them all. I know I saw a great many, but the backgrounds of nearly all of these are dark and confused, still the faces are wonderful. Perhaps when I get older and know more I shall like them better. I got photographs of them all.

The churches are so many that it would be impossible to name them all, and the people seem very devout, and go to church regularly, even if they do go to a bull-fight later. I saw some of the famous pictures painted by Murillo. We saw all the picture galleries, and went through the public gardens and parks, which are very fine and well kept up. There was a grand parade, but what it was for I could not find out, but I think it must have been some sort of religious celebration. I went to visit Señor Sagasta, by appointment, but on account of the fête all the royal family were away, and he had to go with them, so I did not see the baby King of Spain, nor Señor Sagasta either, to my great regret, for I could not remain until they returned to the city. But I saw the palace.

We took a train and went out to the Escurial, which is situated about twenty-five miles from Madrid, and it is said to be one of the most remarkable buildings in the world. It was built by Philip II. of Spain in memory of a victory over the French, and is built on the same plan as St. Peter's at Rome.

There is a gallery of famous paintings and a renowned library, a college and a cloister, and no end of other apartments and rooms. It is set in the midst of rugged mountains, and is built of dark stone. It is surrounded by well kept and beautiful gardens. In the park there are many fountains of the most exquisite workmanship. The monarchs of Spain often spend their summers here, and no one could blame them. The great building has been constructed so as to form hollow courts, and the guide said it was to represent the gridiron on which St. Lawrence was broiled. And the guide said, also, that there were 14,000 doors and 11,000 windows, and the windows are all square, not arched or otherwise decorated. I think the building by far the more impressive, seen from the inside. There seems to be an endless line of galleries and rooms each a part of the general effect. The pictures are rare and fine; but the library struck me most. There is no possibility of counting the rare and remarkable books gathered here, and I hope they are well insured, though no insurance could replace them. I saw an English gentleman light a cigar and throw the lighted match right behind a shelf of books in a very careless manner.

At the Escorial, or Escurial, as some call it, we saw the tombs of several kings, and those of the infantas.

We also saw the Pantheon and the Royal Palace, and visited a monastery, where everything was so strange and silent as to seem almost unreal.

At the Escurial we bought some sweet lemons, the first that I ever saw; but, altogether, I think I never passed such a miserable, unhappy day as that spent there. Everything went wrong, and it was dull, cold and gloomy, and so my remembrance of the Escurial is shrouded in dull clouds.

One of the odd sights in Madrid is to watch the traveling merchants. Each one carries his wares slung all over him. Sometimes it is pots that he sells, of every shape and color. Sometimes chairs and again fruit, or almost anything. The men who sell these things stick to the national costume but many of the fairly well to do, and almost all of those who are well off wear European clothes and the most of the women wear bonnets. There was one man who was fat and red faced who had a basket full of cakes or pies, and another who wandered apparently aimlessly about with a couple of dead rabbits for sale. They sell everything in the streets of Madrid—from things that we would consider entirely worthless to watches and quite fine jewelry and curios. We have plenty of street peddlers, but they do not look picturesque, nor do they lounge against walls that are fairly honeycombed with age, and the stories the guides tell about them. Some of those stories are pretty hard. How many places have been pointed out as ancient prisons where beautiful young princesses and kings and queens have been kept, or perhaps beheaded, I do not know. I lost count of them, but I got the impression that nobody that had royal blood ever died a natural death.

There are a good many gypsies in Madrid, and they are very sharp and shrewd, and if you buy anything of them you are almost sure to be taken in. I did not buy anything of them, but I bought a nice cane for my father, of Toledo make. I did not want to burden myself with a lot of stuff almost in the beginning of my voyage, but I felt sorry afterwards that I did not get some things I wanted and that I could not find after.

Charles and I tramped as we had done at Grenada, and left dear Aunt Mary to rest, as the railway ride and so much sight-seeing were too much for her, still she went around with us a good deal. She was very patient with us though I fear we were noisy and a little crazy with the novelty and pleasure of seeing so many wonders. We wanted her to go and see the bull-fight, but she drew the line right there.

CHAPTER VI.

A BULL-FIGHT IN MADRID.

WHEN you are in Madrid you are expected to see a bull-fight as much as you are to see all the churches and palaces. Indeed if one or the other were to be left unseen it would be the churches, for the bull-fight is considered of far more importance, at least by the Spanish.

Charles and I took a cab and drove to the place where every Sunday at three o'clock they have their bull-fights. This day was a holiday, and on that account the fight took place on Saturday. It was on the outskirts of the city and at the end of one of the principal streets.

BULL-FIGHT AT MADRID.

There is a large amphitheatre which will hold 20,000 persons, and it presents a picturesque sight when full of people,—the women in bright colors, with their black lace mantillas and waving fans. The men are dressed more brilliantly than the women, and all wait impatiently for the fight to begin.

The ring is of sandy earth surrounded by a boarded wall which one might call double, as there is a low one first over which the bull-fighters can jump when too closely pressed, and around the inner one is a narrow platform to aid the men in their leaps to safety. There are large numbers painted on the outer wall, but I do not know what they were for. Above the outer wall are arranged the seats and boxes, that of the king being directly in the centre. We secured seats by the side of the king's box and so had a good view.

The bull-fighters were all dressed in brilliant colors, with much embroidery and gold lace, and they wore their hair in little braided tails or in twists, and they were all very fancy when they went into the ring, but looked pretty dirty and ragged before the fight was ended.

The entrance fee is graduated so that anybody can go, even the very beggars. Women and children go, too, and as soon as mass is over they throng the place, and sit waiting impatiently for the sound of the trumpet which is the sign it is about to begin.

When we arrived the ring was crowded, and as it was too early for the fight the people amused themselves by throwing oranges from the ring to the galleries with sure aim.

The bulls are generally six and chosen, I am told, from nearby places. They are kept for twenty-four hours without food or water and in a dark place.

When the appointed time comes the music plays and the trumpet sounds and a procession of matadors, picadores and espados enter the ring and march around, and as they reach the king's box they take off their hats and salute it whether the king is there or not. Then the key is thrown to the guardian of the gate who unlocks the cage. This time as the door opened there came out a young bull with sharp horns set close together, which are much more deadly than those spreading wider. The men took their places before the bull was fairly in the ring. He dashed forward, half blinded by the light, and there he stood pawing and smelling the the ground. Then he rushed at the nearest matador, but the rush was skillfully dodged by the aid of a large red cloth fluttered before the bull's eyes.

Each matador in turn then teased the bull with the red rag, and as he would make a wild rush at one or the other they would lightly step aside or let him pass under their arms so close that it would make me shudder.

After ten or fifteen minu'es of tormenting the bull, the horses were brought in and mounted by the picadores, who were gorgeously dressed, and carried lances with short spikes.

The horses were the poorest, most miserable looking creatures I ever saw, and they were thin and lame. It is said that something is given them which gives them a semblance of spirit for a little while. They are blindfolded and have the cruel Spanish bit in their mouths, and with all these tortures the poor brutes are spurred on to almost certain death.

The first horse was brought about five yards from the bull who stood looking at him and pawing the ground. Then he charged full on the horse and was received by the mounted picador with a prick from the lance. Sometimes the horse was lifted up over the bull's head, rider and all, but generally the bull gored the horse to death.

The moment the bull would see a horse he would make a dash for him and nearly always manage to catch the horse under the stomach and throw horse and rider over. One rider was hurt and was carried off by two men. I saw ten horses killed in this way by eight bulls, and six bulls killed by the men. The people appeared to enjoy the killing of the horses intensely.

When a horse was too dead to be dragged to his feet with blows or forced to stagger blindly along leaving streams of blood behind him, the bull would be enticed away while the dead horse was dragged out and then it was the bull's own turn to be killed, but he at least has one chance, as he can see as far as the dust and rage will permit.

The matadors would entice the bull away with their red rags, and when he would plunge at them they would dart nimbly aside, and thrust short darts into the bull's neck. They throw six or eight into one bull's neck, making the blood trickle down in streams, and enraging him still more. The horsemen have usually given the bull several prods with the lance before this. Towards the last when he begins to grow exhausted they used darts that were bombs, and these would explode and burst into flame making the poor animal bellow with pain.

Sticking these darts into the bull's neck is one of the hardest and most dangerous things to do. But after a while the bull begins to totter and waver in his motions and foam tinged with blood runs from his mouth, and then the last act in the drama of his life begins. The man whose business it is to finish the killing of the bull stands off a few yards and begins lifting his arms up and down until the bull with his eyes bloodshot and his tongue hanging out makes one final rush forward and charges upon the man, who lightly steps aside and reaches over the bull's horns and places two darts one in each shoulder, hampering the bull's movements. Then the espado steps forward with his short, sharp sword and red rag teasing the wretched creature until he finds his weakest point, and watching his chance plunges the sword into the neck, and if the blow be a true one, and it generally is, the bull falls dead as if struck by lightning.

As soon as the last shiver has passed over the bull the espado jumps upon the body and stabs it once or twice more and then strikes a circus attitude while the people go wild, and shout and throw bouquets, cigars and hats into the ring. The espado throws the hats back but the rest are his own. It is said that people often throw him jewels and other valuables, but that I did not see.

As soon as two or three horses and one bull are killed, more are brought in, and the same thing is repeated with little variation. Some bulls have very little fight in them, and the people shout to " kill him " and such have little mercy. The people judge of the success of the bull-fight by the number of decrepit horses mangled and killed, and I heard that not long ago there was very nearly a revolution because there were not horses enough killed in the fights.

After the horses and bulls were all killed, they let in a young bull with covered horns, and all the gamins were permitted to go in the ring against him, and he tossed them around to his heart's content to the great delight of the people, who seem to look upon this as the farce after the tragedy.

Aside from the bull-fights there are theatres, and the public promenades on the Prado of afternoons by way of amusements in Madrid, and also operas in season. The Spanish love music very much, and it seems as if every one can play on the guitar and sing.

CHAPTER VII.

BURGOS TO THE RIVIERA.

WE left for Burgos, on our way across the Pyrenees to France, after a most wretched day. It was cold and windy, and there was nothing to do but wait for the train which left at 12.30 that night, and therefore made but a short stay in that city; but we visited several points of interest, among them the Town Hall, where they keep the bones of the Cid in a case. There is a castle which was built in 895 A. D., and it is very interesting to those who love antiquities. Every foot of ground and every great building is more or less historic in Spain, and worthy of careful study.

When we were on our way across the great chain of mountains I felt really sad to leave Spain with her almost universal look of past glories, and pass over the snow-clad Pyrenees into France.

Perhaps it was my imagination, but I felt sure that the landscape wore a lighter, trimmer look. Wherever we passed a farm or village everything was clean and neat and the people were at work, instead of lounging around, smoking vile black cigars. Really, laziness is brought to a fine art in Spain, and if the Moors hadn't built these grand old edifices I don't believe there would have ever been any Spain, but now the people have to live up to them to a certain degree.

Along towards dark we began to come from under the shadow of those great mountains and draw near Pau, and I think I was never more glad than when we arrived at that beautiful place. We passed several farms near that famous health resort, and I saw cows. Here, I thought, one can venture on a good glass of milk—and later I did. There was no chalk there nor water, and how good the milk was!

I cannot describe the grand and beautiful scenery on the way from Burgos to Pau. It was wild and savage in some parts and peaceful and charming in others, but some of the mountain peaks were simply terrible—they were so rugged and barren. We spun around the mountains and across trestle bridges in a manner to make your hair curl, and I never expect to see so grand and sublime a sight again as the heart of the Pyrenees. It must have been something of an undertaking in the old days to march an army through and over these rugged mountains and wild gorges.

Pau is at the foot of these great snow-covered mountains, and from one window

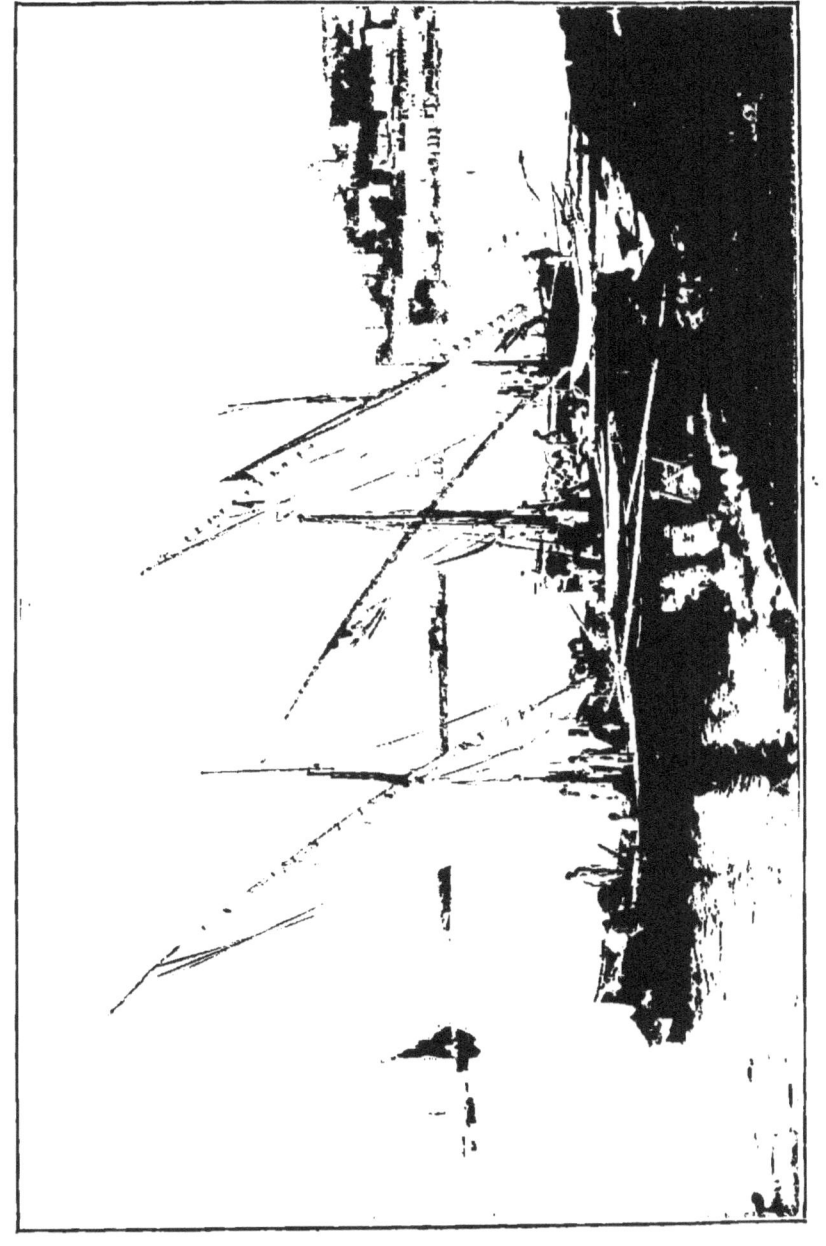

CANNES.

you can look from the hotel and count the high white peaks, and from the other you can see the low and pleasant country where it is like a garden. Many Americans gather at Pau in the winter. From Pau we went to Cannes, passing through Marseilles and Toulouse.

We were two hours only in Marseilles, and had little time to see anything, but what I did I liked very much. The people all seemed busy and active. The French people are workers by nature and very neat and clean. We saw many foreigners in their national costumes, and suppose they belonged to the ships, which gathered there from all countries. The stores are so neat and orderly that it is a pleasure to see them. The Canebiere is something worth seeing, for there is more business done there in an hour than anywhere else in Europe. They say in Marseilles that if Paris had a Canebiere it would be nearly as good as a little Marseilles.

From Marseilles we went on to Toulouse, where we spent the evening, but saw next to nothing there, as our time was so limited. We reached Cannes the last day of March, and started for Nice four days later. Cannes is an interesting city, and is most beautifully situated on the shores of a curving bay, and is built up on the hill-side. In the distance can be seen a dim line of mountains, and there are always many sailing boats drawn up along the shore, with what I believe they call lateen sails, which look far too big for the boats. The old part of the city is very interesting with a style of architecture new to us, and quaint and romantic.

There are a great many semi-tropical plants there that made it seem very pleasant, particularly along the Boulevard de la

Croisette. This is a wide and well paved street, extending along the bay and bordered with palm trees. Along the upper side of this street are handsome houses with fine gardens with luxuriant flowers and trees, and between all the houses are green trees and creeping vines.

There are many invalids in Cannes, and many very nice hotels to receive them. There are pleasant sails around the bay, and drives around the outskirts of the city, and a magnificent view of a large tract of beautiful country lying below the top of quite a high hill upon which one portion of the city is built.

There are the usual number of churches and other places of general interest to see, but I cannot now recall what they were. I only know that we liked Cannes, and that it had a restful air about it, and that no one seems to care very much about working while there. The scenery is not wild, but the old part of the town is picturesque, both from a distance and when in it. I think the rest there did Aunt Mary good, and I know it did me, and I gave up to it all I could.

From there we went to Nice where we stayed about a week. It is no wonder so many persons go there, and afterwards forget that there is any other place in the world. All you want to do is to wander about and see the strange faces of people from everywhere, many of them Americans and English. The people from these two countries, I think, must just about support Nice. It has a very even climate and the sun shines nearly always, so that many persons with weak chests go there. The gardens around are pleasant and the trees are semi-tropical with many palms and other plants that give Nice the air of a hot-house built out-doors. The hotel where we stayed fronts the bay,

and from the windows one has a splendid picture painted by nature i self. The Promenade des Anglaises is a fine street, and at all hours you will see people riding or walking along and making the most of the pleasant hours.

Cannes, Nice, Monte Carlo, and Mentone, are so near together that it is a pleasant and not tiresome trip to go from one to another. Aunt Mary was so tired that she preferred to rest, and so Charles and I started from Nice to Monte Carlo on bicycles, where we had hoped to see the famous gambling place.

We rode along the Cornichi roadway nine miles. This is a smooth and excellent road, built by Napoleon, very steep, and it lies along the sea, often shut on one side by high cliffs, and in two or three places it goes through a tunnel, or arch of rock. The ride that day is one that I shall long remember. The blue sky was reflected in the still water, which was so clear that we could see every pebble, and we saw lovely flowers growing in the crevices of the rocks above us. There is a stone wall nearly breast-high along the sea edge of this fine road.

We reached Monte Carlo tired and dusty, and looked too disreputable to be permitted to enter the gambling hall at Monaco. So we consoled ourselves by strolling around and admiring the surroundings. It seems as if everything that human minds could invent in the way of beautiful surprises had been put in that place. Rare flowers and plants, fountains and statues, winding walks and fancy seats and little kiosks were everywhere. We saw many people wandering around but nearly all had their eyes turned towards the promontory where the great gambling hall was. Later we all came to Monte Carlo and spent a whole afternoon

MENTONE, THE "OLD CITY."

and evening, and the elder members of the party went into the great hall to see the gambling. No one is admitted who is under 21. We drove about the place which has been made one of the most enticing places in the world, and all this has been paid for out of the money lost at the gaming tables.

Charles and I were very hungry after our long ride that day and as we were to return we thought we would have some refreshment and ordered everything we wanted, but when we came to pay our bill it took every cent we had with us, and did not leave anything for the waiter, and he was so angry that one would have thought he had been wilfully defrauded of a million dollars. On the way I think we met every beggar in the country, and after giving to the first ones all we could spare we had to hurry past the rest, looking up at the clinging vines and pretending not to see their outstretched hands. Some of them were really pitiful objects. One man I saw without legs, and another a hunchback dwarf. They are of all ages, from little children who will drop their playthings and run after travelers for small coins, and return to play, if they are fortunate or unlucky, with the same spirit. There are old beggars whose wrinkled faces and round backs tell of much hardship, and there are no end of blind and lame beggars. No person could give them all money. Nearly all were barefooted, and two or three times I felt an impulse to give some of them a card which would have been good for a pair of shoes in New York. I don't see how it is that there are so many beggars abroad that make a regular business of it. Who gives them enough to live on, and how do they live? Does there not come a day when no one gives them anything and they simply die of hunger or do they get used to living without food. I do not know, but this I do know, the sight of so much suffering was like a perpetual reproach to me. I cannot understand how God creates some people to suffer want and misery all their whole lives, and they are good people, too, and others have so much that they cannot begin to enjoy a thousandth part of it. But, He knows and it must be right.

After we had left Monte Carlo we went to Genoa.

CHAPTER VIII.

GENOA.

*O*F Nice and Cannes, Mentone and Monte Carlo are beautiful Genoa is interesting. We passed through that city going to Pisa, and Florence, and stayed there some days on our return and so I shall put all I saw there in one chapter.

The harbor of Genoa is not large but the commerce is, and the ships and steamers and smaller craft are warped in in a wonderful manner, and they lay so close to each other that parties visit other vessels just as we might call on a next door neighbor. The harbor is protected by the moles, or we would call them bulkheads,

THE CORNICHI ROAD.

but it makes it safe for shipping in heavy storms.

Genoa is not a very pretty city close to it or when in it. The houses in some of the old streets are so high and the streets so narrow that they are slimy and smell musty, for the sun never gets in. When the founders of this city begun it they had all outdoors to build on, and it is hard to understand how it was that they made such narrow streets. I know some are not over six feet wide. Down in these narrow streets are many shops, particularly of the filagree workers, and the mosaic makers, and I think relic and coin factories, where relics and old coins are skilfully imitated to be sold to foreigners, who are their legitimate prey. Some of the silver and gold filagree is very beautiful and finely wrought. I think filagree work is a specialty with the Genoese. Some of it looks like the tracings of frost on the windows.

All along the port there is a wide quay, which is the chosen promenade of all the Genoese and there are many more of them than the size of the city would lead one to expect. I liked to watch them walk slowly along, and in fact, I saw no one in a hurry while there. Everything is "piano-piano" there, even the stevedores on the dock taking things easy.

Genoa is built on seven hills, and there has been little attempt at grading the streets except in the most modern part. The old houses nearly all have stucco ornaments. The newer ones are quite fine. Some of the palaces of the ancient nobility are interesting to see, and become still more so as you listen to the wildly romantic histories given them by the guides. Nearly all have trees and gardens wherever it is possible, and the

SAN REMO, SEEN FROM THE MOLE.

parks and public gardens are very fine and clean. They have fine music in one of these parks evenings. There are 212,000 inhabitants and they are all music lovers. How many palaces there are I cannot tell, as I think we saw some of them more than once, but there were many and all fine buildings. And there are several, I think ten, forts and a wall and ramparts. This was the first time I had ever seen a fortified city, and it struck me very much, and the fortifications were more interesting to me than anything else.

There are many churches, and in most of them were fine paintings, among them several by Rubens, who, they tell you lived in Genoa awhile, and there were other famous paintings, some in churches and some in the private palaces where they allow visitors at certain hours during the day.

Of course, we hear all about Cristofero Colombo, and are dragged around through narrow streets and decayed houses to see this or that thing that had had some connection with the man that gave us the greatest country in the world, and at last as the crowning sight we were hauled up before the monument the Genoese have had erected in the plaza before the railway station—the Plaza Aquaverde. It is a large and beautiful statue and has a pedestal that is covered with allegorical figures, representing wisdom, science, geography, strength, and religion. The statue is of marble, and Columbus leans on an anchor, and at the foot of the statue is a figure representing America waiting to be discovered. Between the figures mentioned above there are bas reliefs representing scenes on the voyage of Columbus. All around the statue are palm trees and a beautiful park. There is a palace almost opposite with marble carvings also representing scenes from the life of Columbus.

The streets of Genoa are very interesting, particularly those where you can take long drives. One of them leads up and around the fortifications, and winds among the hills and up and down them, and past the poor house which has space for 1300 persons, and is always full. Another leads down along the shore and from there the city looks its best. Another leads outside of the city to the great camphor tree gardens, we did not know about that until too late to go and see it, but it is said to be very interesting to see.

The royal palace is a handsome building and it is open daily for the people to see the pictures and statues and the rooms, which are magnificently furnished. It is only while the royal family is absent that strangers are allowed to go through them.

I remember that we took one drive back of the city, along a low stretch of country that was made very interesting by the picturesque appearance of the people. The ground was low and for the most part marshy, and it was here that I saw people getting peat for the first time. These peat beds are said to be the largest known. They shave off the surface of the soggy ground, and cut it into squares and dry it, and burn it instead of wood. It is said to give a clear, steady flame with very little smoke. It struck me as being an improvement on our way of getting fuel, as you do not have to mine, chop or saw this.

The Campo Santo was just beyond these peat beds, and the grave-stones looked like so many little houses. The Campo Santo is the burial ground of the wealthy and distinguished Genoese, and resembles Westminster Abbey in that respect. Some of the sculpture on the tombs is very beautiful, but some of the carvings look like designs made and carried out by some little child. They

THE HARBOR OF GENOA.

are simply awful. We walked all around the galleries and saw all the tombs of note, but we felt rather depressed and disappointed in some ways, as we had been led to expect wonders. Perhaps if we had known the histories of the people buried there we might have felt more interested in their tombs, and it is very depressing to walk about in a cemetery anyhow.

CHAPTER IX.

PISA.

PRONTO, Pronto, came from all along the line of guards, and click, click came from the locks, and we moved off towards Pisa from Genoa. We passed through 85 tunnels between the two cities, catching at times glimpses of snow-clad mountains, lovely valleys, and queer little towns as we rode along. We had stopped over night at Genoa, and now were on our way again. After nearly four miserable hours we arrived at Pisa. The Duomo and the Leaning Tower were plainly visible as we approached, but on entering the city we soon lost sight of those two land-marks that have been famous so many generations.

As we passed through the city gates our belongings were examined to be sure that we had nothing dutiable, and as we had not we were allowed to go in. I wonder what they would have done if we had any.

The hotel we stopped at was on the right bank of the Arno along which is the principal street of Pisa. Pisa is a small but ancient city with about 38,000 inhabitants. The Cathedral, the Leaning Tower, and Campo Santo are spoken of as the great points of interest and to see them all tourists go, but I found very many more things to see that interested me. The old and quaint architecture, the dark faces of the majority of the people, the air of being very far behind the times, the queer little shops, the keen, sharp faces of the children, and the hopeless drooping visages of the old people, and the general "take life easy" air of all others, were like so many living pictures to carry away in my mind.

The next day after our arrival we procured a guide, and put ourselves into his hands unconditionally, and let him lead us where he would. He took us first, as in duty bound, to see what is called the finest group of buildings in the world. The Cathedral forms a Latin cross, both outside and in. There is a platform of five steps of marble, and the bronze doors are most beautiful.

As we entered the door a blind beggar began his pitiful wail of "meurs de faim," until he received some money. I tried to harden my heart all I could to the persistent and often impudent demands of all sorts of beggars, but there is something so dismal in the thought of a man shut in the darkness and holding out his hand for help that may or may not come, and which he cannot seek in any other way, that if all the beggars I saw had been blind, I should have had to hold out my own hand too.

The Cathedral is so cold that one feels as if he had got into an ice house and it chilled me through so that I had to leave as soon as I possibly could. In the Nave there is a large bronze lamp suspended from the ceiling, and this, the guide tells you without winking, was what gave Galileo the idea of a pendulum, and then he pokes it with a stick to make it swing.

You must try and pretend to believe all the guide says, if you want to hear all the stories he tells to give new interest to the things he shows. I believe some of our guides could pick up a paving stone and wind such a story around it that you would almost get down on your knees to it with reverence for such a wonderful thing. Every inch of wall and every hole in the ground has some remarkable history, and the guides tell you all about it, and they use so many gestures and words that I think they must die young, worn out by their efforts.

Guides are not the poorest people in these places by any means. They usually have a lot of relics to sell secretly, and they stand in with nearly all the storekeepers and get you to buy many things you really do not want. The guide persuades, grieves, bullies if he thinks he can, until he gets you to a place where there is something to sell, and then he gives the merchant a wink to show you are a "tenderfoot," and afterwards he gets his commission. Some of the guides are meek and never say no, but others domineer, not only over the travelers, but over everyone around, for on the guide depends the liberality of the traveler, and they levy tribute everywhere.

It would be a hopeless task to try to tell all the beauties of the Cathedral, and we left there with regret, in spite of the cold atmosphere, and crossed over to the Baptistery, which is a wonderful structure, entirely of marble. It is circular, with a conical dome 190 feet high. I think it a finer thing than the Leaning Tower. The carving is lavish and fine, and the interior is very imposing; and the effect of the stained glass windows was very beautiful, as the colored lights fall upon the rich sculptures. The keeper sang for us and his fine voice was echoed back from a hundred points, making the vast dome ring with the music.

The next place of interest we visited was the Campo Santo or burial ground. This is a long building Tuscan-Gothic style. In the middle is a large open court in which 53 loads of holy soil from Mount Calvary were put, in order that the dead might repose in holy earth.

The Campo Santo is filled with old sarcophagi, frescoes, paintings and carvings, and the old chains of the harbor of Pisa are hung on the walls. We were led to a corner of the grounds from whence we could see the Leaning Tower, the Cathedral, and the Baptistery all in one wonderful picture, outlined against the deep blue sky. A visit to the Campo Santo, the guide said, would be very impressive, but we found it more curious and interesting than impressive. We picked some flowers there, and gathered up a little of the soil to keep.

The Leaning Tower came next and after paying the entrance fee, which has to be paid everywhere, to see anything except the churches, we mounted the steps, 294 I believe, and did not find it very difficult, as you feel as if you were going down part of the time. We reached the top and from there had a fine view of the city, its environs, mountains, and the sea. It was worth climbing twice as high to see the lovely picture spread out there before us.

In the tower there are six bells, the heaviest weighing six tons, and this hangs on the upper or higher side, so it could not have been that which caused the tower to slant over. The tower slants 13 feet out of the perpendicular. It is 179 feet high, and the guide told us Galileo experimented with this also, regarding the laws of gravitation. The guide never heard of Newton.

It is thought by some that the tower sunk while in the course of construction and the top was added as it is, on that account. It was commenced 719 years ago and finished 543 years since. I think that some architect did this to order for some ruler that wanted to have an oddity to show strangers and get perpetual fees for, and if this is so he "builded better than he knew," for the sum paid in fees for 543 years must have amounted to a tidy sum.

Some members of our party went to a sculptor's and bought some statuary, and we all bought some photographs, and on our return to the hotel we arranged our plans for the next morning, and decided to go on to Florence.

CHAPTER X.

FLORENCE.

WE passed through many tunnels on the way from Pisa to Florence, which made it a very hot and dusty ride, and we were tired enough on reaching Florence to rest well that night, but to my intense delight I met two of my American friends as we entered the dining room for dinner, and we sat up till nearly morning talking and comparing notes, for they were to leave the next day.

Florence was full of strangers, as it was just at the time the Queen of England was there, and one or two of the Indian princes, besides the Prince of Bulgaria. You could not look in any direction without seeing some great personage.

The next morning I went for a drive with my American lady friend and we went to the Cascine, the fashionable promenade, and we enjoyed our ride greatly as Florence is a most beautiful city, and there are many things worth seeing. My friends left Florence that afternoon for Venice, and I was very sorry for it feels good to meet old friends in strange lands.

We took rooms at the New York Hotel, and were very glad to get such good ones as the city was so crowded, and yet I feel as if justice will not have done all she ought to until she gives that hotel-keeper a good shaking. He persuaded me to buy a dog of his cousin, a "real St. Bernard, the smooth-coated, brindled kind." They told me that the fat little puppy that they showed me was born in Switzerland, and how badly the monks had felt to let him go, and how the race was dying out and that only the need of money to carry on their monastery where so many perishing travelers were saved and cared for, would force these good brothers to sell one; "it was like parting with a child," etc., and I took it all in like a dutiful American, and bought the pup. He was seven weeks old and had a knowing little face, and he seemed to take to me at once. I will not tell the trouble he made me, nor the tricks he played, nor the valuables he chewed up, I prefer to think of what jolly comrades we became. I called him Selim, and got him a collar and chain. One day Charles and I went out and left him with the cook, who gave him so much to eat that he was nearly as round as a ball, and cried all night with the colic, like a baby. But I grew very fond of him. The hotel-keeper and his deceptive cousin said that Selim would be as big as a calf when he was three months old. I will dismiss the subject by saying that the dog proved to be a brindled terrier, and never grew much bigger but he is a thoroughbred of his kind. But I bought him for a St. Bernard and paid accordingly. I suppose that instead of praying for anything else in the way of good fortune these men just ask to have another fool American come along.

Our first visit to the picture galleries was made the next day after our arrival and we went to the Ufizzi and Pitti palaces which were joined by a long corridor, and one can see them both in one day. It is said that Florence has one of the finest collections of pictures gathered in one place in the world.

Michael Angelo, Murillo, Raphael and Andre de Sarto all have their finest works gathered here.

The pictures are portioned off according to the different schools, Flemish, Italian and others. The tribune is the finest room in the Ufizzi palace, and Raphael, Titian and Fra Angelico have made it a gem. There are also many choice pieces of statuary, and frescoes, and it is an education of the eye to different kinds of beauty to see them.

The Ufizzi Palace is near the Plaza Signorie and is above the post office. Long halls on three sides are filled with ancient sculptures and paintings, one room for the most ancient gems of painting, another for old statuary, and various other things. From these halls are doors which lead into the so-called treasure chambers in which are the most valuable pictures. These rooms are generally filled with young artists who are vainly trying to outdo the great works of the Masters.

One very long passage-way connects the Ufizzi Palace and the Pitti, and in that are about 500 paintings by noted artists. The rooms are divided off and called after the names of different gods, as the Salon of Jupiter, Salon of Mars, etc.

The palace is the largest ever built by a private family and the stones are all rugged on the outside, the edges where they join only have been smoothed.

The reception rooms are furnished in the most splendid manner. From the courtyard extend the beautiful Boboli Gardens. On certain days of the week these gardens are open to the public, and crowds come to enjoy the magnificent view from these grottos, and fountains are everywhere. From one spot near the top we obtained a view of all the city, including the Dome, the Campanile of the Cathedral Palecchio and tower of the Budia. These grounds are so extensive that it takes a long time to explore all. There is an old amphitheatre where both public and private performances were given, but now it is used for such solemn ceremonies as it is desired to have in public.

The steps and laundry have sculptures such as Perseus, the head of Medusa in bronze, and others in marble. After we had seen all these we went through the narrow streets of the town, out on the Lungarno, along several bridges until we came to the Ponte Vecchio. This old bridge is crowded with small jewelry shops, much like the Rialto of Venice.

It was late in the afternoon so we returned to the hotel, and it was suggested that we take a carriage the next morning and just see everything we could reach in one day, so as soon as breakfast was over we started. We drove by the Stuzza Palace where the noted bronze lamps hang and thence around to the Duomo and the Baptistery on which are the wonderful bronze doors, and from there we went to the Campanile and the

Cathedral. I could not tell anything about these places that has not been told hundreds of times better than I could tell it, and I shall not disgrace myself trying.

We then went to the Palazzio del Signorina, and on to the old palace and the Loggia del Lanze, the Palazzio delle Ufizzi, the National library and several other places of note. The Loggia del Lanze is a magnificent open vault.

The Ufizzi palace galleries hold some of the most beautiful statuary and pictures in the world, and there is not a yard of space that does not show some piece of sculpture or painting that is worth the whole trip to see. The very roofs of the long galleries and the round room and the smaller rooms are all beautifully decorated. That is where the foreigners are ahead of us. Their houses are simply big pictures with sculptured settings. There is hardly any building of any pretension that is not richly ornamented this way. There are so many beautiful statues around the city, and magnificent fountains and other works of art, that I cannot begin to remember them all, but they make Florence a beautiful city.

When we crossed the river and came around on the other side, and back to the hotel, and after lunch we rode up the Via del Coli, to Piazzalo Michael Angelo, and passed St. Miniato. The Piazzalo Michael Angelo is on the top and side of one of the hills back of Florence and it affords a splendid view, and from there Florence looks as though it was in a cup. Fiesole and St. Croce are on neighboring hills on the opposite side. The country around is beautiful, not so grand as parts of Spain but very pleasing. Florence is like a picture set in a green frame, and on a clear day you can pick out towns and churches for miles around. There is a little restaurant up there where you can get a lunch that tastes very good after such a long drive.

The next day after this trip everybody was expected to get up about four o'clock, and gather in the mall of the Cacheani and prepare their breakfasts on the wooden tables. It was "Concepcion day." Hundreds of men and boys went around with tiny cages in each of which was a cricket, which had been caught the night before. These were eagerly bought by those who had not caught any for themselves. The boys and men would poke straws down the crickets' nests and make them come out only to be caged. They were supposed to bring good luck to the owners. It seemed that all the people in Florence were out at half-past four, rich and poor, natives and strangers to laugh and chat and show each other their little black captives.

It was my good fortune to see the famous procession of flowers, and it was a brilliant spectacle. The city was all excitement, and the cab men doubled their price for that day. Peddlers charged extra for their wares, and the flower sellers reaped golden harvests.

All the royalty were to take part in it, with their best carriages, each decked with flowers. All the people who could afford to hire a carriage of any kind put a few, or a good many flowers on horse and carriage and entered the procession.

A special stand had been erected for the Queen of England, and all the palaces had their private stands for themselves and friends. The streets were crowded with spectators, and as we gazed down at them from our window it seemed as if all Italy had crowded out to see the celebration.

We were right opposite the Stuzzi Palace, on which are the famous lanterns, but the massive blocks of stone give it such a dreary look from the outside no one could imagine that one of the oldest families in Italy lived there in such imperial magnificence.

All the balconies were filled with flowers to throw at the passers, and everybody carried at least one bunch. As we looked up and down the street it seemed as if a luxuriant garden had suddenly sprung up, and it was beautiful.

All this time carriages went hurrying to and fro, loaded with lovely flowers, probably to fall in the line of the procession. Then the police came along on horseback, and the thoroughfare was closed, and so were the side streets, so that the procession could pass. The crowds were not kept in very good order, but they were good natured, and no disturbance occurred.

The people have a great fear of the police who are generally mounted, and are nearly all fine looking men, but what the police have, in the way of good looks, the soldiers sadly lack, for the most of them are little bits of fellows about four feet five or six inches tall, and have no war-like air or appearance that I could discern.

The procession started at last headed by a cab, with some lilacs on the horses' head, and then followed a whole string of cabs like the first with very few flowers, and scarcely any were exchanged with the people on foot or in the windows.

Then came the royal carriages with their gorgeous liveried footmen in white wigs. One of these carriages was covered entirely with lilies of the valley, from the hubs of the wheels to the ends of the harness, and on the back was the coat of arms of the owner who was seated in the carriage. Now the battle began in earnest. Flowers began to fly from balconies, and from the crowds, and the bombardment was returned from the carriages. One carriage was a mass of white roses with red ones around the sides and tire of the wheels. Another was covered with daisies.

Behind all these finely gotten up carriages were the footmen who tried to keep the populace from touching the flowers, but the crowds of boys were not afraid of the footmen and dodged the driver's whips and made sad havoc of the decorations.' Close carriages followed, covered with violets, calla lilies and roses, and some had no flowers at all, but the people in them caught the flowers that flew thickly through the air. Everybody laughed, or shouted, and dodged flowers or threw them, so that it was like a garden in the air.

The procession turned in the square and came back so that there was a line going and coming, and as they passed each other more flowers flew back and forth from carriage to carriage. It was a pretty sight, but I could not help thinking what a funny thing it would be in New York. I hardly think our American aristocracy would look right in such a procession.

The Queen of England had a special stand to sit on and see the parade, and crowds gathered around it to catch a glimpse of her. Some threw flowers up to her, and all waited patiently in the hope of catching a flower that she might throw. There were a few fortunate enough to get them.

The bands of music had been playing all day at the public squares, and as it grew late they stopped, and the people dispersed, leaving the street strewn with crushed flowers. The stores, and in fact all business was closed and we went home to rest.

The Brothers of the Misericordia are one of the sights in Florence. They are all men usually of good family who devote their lives to the work of burying the dead and caring for the injured in any accident, or taking the sick to hospitals. They wear long, black habits and with a hood over the face having holes to see through, they look like ghosts. They carry the sick in a sort of basket and the dead in a coffin covered with a black pall, on their shoulders. One walks in front of them with his face uncovered. When they pass all the people cross themselves and say a short prayer for the sick or the dead. It is said that the last grand Duke was a member of this brotherhood, and that when the cholera raged there he worked with the rest. Some of the poorer people also join the Misericordia and the

THE BROTHERS OF THE MISERICORDIA.

guide says you can tell a gentleman from a peasant by the feet. They do a noble and self-sacrificing work.

One evening there was a torchlight review of soldiers, and a civic parade together in honor of the Queen of England. She was seated on a balcony surrounded by her suite and some princes and other notables. The parade was very fine and some of the floats and transparencies were very ingenious. There were all sorts of animals and fishes, and a locomotive and cars. It was beautiful indeed, when it passed the Duomo and front of the great Cathedral, as the lights reflected upon them in such a way that it looked like a fairy scene.

The streets were lined with people, and the crowd so great that it was not possible to cross the street. I had been out for a walk with my little dog, and as the crowd was so dense, I was afraid he would get hurt and took him up in my arms. He was a very affectionate little puppy and there was a lady standing close to me. Selim managed to get his nose up and licked her face, and she turned on me like a flash, thinking I had done it. I showed her the dog and made her understand that he did it, and she was madder than ever, and I seized a chance to get back to the hotel.

Aunt Mary was taken quite ill with so much fatigue and decided to remain in Florence while Charles and I were to go to Naples and Rome and a few other places, and, though we went for the sake of giving her the quiet and rest she needed I felt very uneasy and afraid, but she was in such good hands that we finally overcame our scruples and started with the pup.

CHAPTER XI.

NAPLES.

WE reached Naples late at night and engaged rooms at the Grand Hotel which we supposed was near the depot, but it was quite a quarter of an hour's ride. We went to bed at once, and were up the next morning bright and early, and I think I was about two hours dressing, for every minute I would drop everything and look out of the window. There was Vesuvius smoking away in the distance, across the water and beyond a sketch of green country. I cannot tell how strange it seemed to have geography come to life like that. The bay was beautiful near by and shadowy and purple in the distance, and the little boats with their wing-like sails glided along like birds. There were ships and steamers there, too, and when the sun rose over the distant hills it made them all look as if they were standing up out of the water. The smoke from the volcano floated slowly on the breeze, and it seemed that there never could be so lovely a place anywhere else in the world.

The wide Boulevard below was full of marine soldiers, drilling for the fete, which was to celebrate the coming of the Emperor of Germany, and in fact the whole city seemed full of them.

There were many war vessels, one of the largest ones afloat among them. The night before, when we arrived they had been surveying the city by their powerful search lights and some of the people went nearly frantic with fear at first. I suppose they thought Vesuvius had broken forth in a new spot, but soon they were quieted and the shore was crowded with people to see the wonder.

At last I was dressed and it being Sunday we went to church, which we were nearly an hour finding, for no one could or would tell where it was, and we finally engaged a cab for two francs, and found that it was less than one square away, and while we were bargaining with the driver we were the center of an inquisitive and interested group, who watched the whole proceding with the greatest pleasure, if we could judge by their looks.

After service we returned to the hotel for lunch, and found it hard to console little Selim for my absence. He whined and rolled around and tried to tell me how lonesome he had been, for I had left him in the room. He was so young that he was a lot of trouble but I was very fond of him. He would not walk with a chain on if he could help it, but would sit down and brace himself back and howl, but he had to get used to it, and did after a while. As soon as he was comfortably disposed for a nap we started on a long drive on the hill. We had a splendid horse and he did noble work climbing the hills. The road was winding, and very dusty, but what splendid views we had of the beautiful Bay of Naples, with all its outlying towns, Castlemarre, Sorrento and others spread out like a picture.

Every now and then we would get glimpses of Capri, and a far-away sight of the smoking mountain, which would every few minutes send up a succession of puffs, and once in a while a small shower of stones. The smoke would be sometimes a thin little line, and the next minute perhaps, there would be a heavy volume of black smoke. It fascinated me as nothing else had.

VIEW OF NAPLES.

On the summit of the ridge of hills there is a road which runs all along out to the end of the promontory, and this gives a changing panorama of the Mediterranean and numbers of small towns nestled in valleys. On the side farthest from Naples the hills sloped down to low, marshy land covered with cypress trees, but there were some cultivated places. We could also see the Island of Ischia.

The driver took us a long way and at last came to the so-called wonderful Grotto de Cannes, which was down on our list as one of the sights to see. We descended into a little valley where we were shown a list of prices, but we paid no attention to them as it was all a fraud.

We were first shown through a curious low doorway into a hall, and as soon as we entered we became aware that the temperature had risen considerably, and we also became conscious that we were walking over a hollow place, and our guide took up a large sledge and struck the ground and it sounded like striking an empty wooden box.

Fumes of sulphur came out from all over the floor and walls and I put my hand over a little hole from which fumes were coming, but I quickly drew it back, and blew on my fingers, for it was red hot. This place proved to be an old Roman bath, and the old stone beds were pointed out to us where the lazy Romans used to repose while taking their hot bath.

We explored until we began to get decidedly warm, so we went outside and were conducted to a little stone building and the guide insisted that we should enter, and then he told us to put our heads down, which we did, but drew them back together as the ground was highly charged with magnesian oxide, and it was so powerful that it would kill a person in a very short time. He then led us to the Grotto de Cannes, through a low door-way, but he held us back, saying that we must go no further. He lit a torch and put it down to the ground and it was extinguished immediately, from the presence of carbonic acid gas, and pointing to the wall he showed us how high the gas reached by a black mark all around the wall as high as the gas mounted. He took up a bucket and dipped it full of this gas just as you would water and proved the presence of the gas by the fact that nothing would burn in it. A small dog was then dragged in, and where a man might stand with safety, his head above the gas, the dog's head was in it, and in a few minutes he was staggering around and coughing. He was taken out, but after staggering around a little he fell as if dead, but he soon revived and seemed to be as well as ever. I put my head down into the gas a little, and instantly felt as though my breath had been checked.

In olden times it is said that they put criminals in here to kill them, I wonder who could have built the stairway which leads down to the bottom. I did not care to explore in the hope of finding out.

The guide took a torch and lit it and then wet it a little and blew it out to make smoke which settled on top of the carbonic acid gas, and it looked just like a mirror lake.

The visit to this place gave us a greater desire to visit Vesuvius. As we left the guide to the Grotto made a demand for twice as much as he had agreed upon, but we gave him just what we had promised, and he shook his fist at us, and called us all sorts of things in Italian.

Coming back we made arrangements to go to Vesuvius the next morning, and the driver promised to be on hand early. Returning to Naples, we went through an old Roman tunnel which went under the hill we had gone over in the morning. It was at least half a mile long, and was filled with wagons and people passing from Naples to and from the neighboring towns.

We hurried the next morning to get ready for what was, to me, the greatest trip I ever made: to Pompeii and Mount Vesuvius. We had the same horse that we had had the day before and he was a good one, and how he did step out!

We were not long in leaving Naples behind and we passed through several little fishing towns, where the people seemed to be doing nothing but sit around or rise slowly to look at us as we rode by. There were racks all along the roadside, hung full of macaroni drying in the sun, and among these racks children played, and donkeys and pigs walked about as if it was a garden full of weeds, instead of something people were to eat after. The people were dirty beyond my power to describe and the most of the men had sullen faces and the women were not pretty. In fact they looked much like the Italians we see around New York.

The streets of Naples are paved with great blocks of hard lava, dark in color, and many of the houses, particularly those of the poorer quarters are built of lava and other volcanic material, fastened together with some kind of cement. The whole city, as you look back at it from a rise in the road looks like an amphitheater, and is more beautiful than words can tell. The bay curves in, and every wave-washed point has something new to show, that cannot be seen anywhere else. The little villages along the edges of the hills, are half hidden in vines and trees, and there are several monasteries looking like fortresses standing in gloomy stateliness on prominent places.

It is about four miles from Naples to the foot of the Volcano, and we passed through seven or eight small hamlets before we reached a straight and quiet road, but there was a layer of fine white dust four or five inches thick which flew into the air in clouds and nearly suffocated us. Once in a while it would blow off so that we could get a glimpse of the smoking crater. The driver would stop from time to time and point out old ruins where once had been fine homes, and great heaps of lava and scoria which looked like the coke thrown out of fire engines.

At last we reached a little inn, where they have saddle horses to mount the Volcano with, and we went into the place to engage a guide. There were so many that we hardly knew what to do, but finally we engaged one to take us through the ruins of Pompeii, as we were told that we would have time to visit that place before dinner. So we bought our tickets and started for the buried city, which is now being slowly dug out of the earth where it has been hidden so many years. Our guide was a Spaniard who had lived in America for some time, and he took advantage of that fact to charge us about double for his services.

We entered Pompeii by the Marine Gate, which is the gate that led out of the city to the seashore where the ancients used to take their boats. Pompeii was a walled city and now nearly all the wall has been traced. Entering the Marine Gate we went first to the Museum where they have collected all the things that have been found during the excavations. There were things truly wonderful. There were loaves of bread that had been found in an oven that had been sealed up by dried mud and lava all these centuries. There were raisins and all sorts of dried fruit and pretty dry, too, and kernels of wheat, and there were any amount of lamps of every description, from clay to silver and bronze, and there were many exquisitely formed vases, of every size, kitchen utensils, a portable stove, statues and some mural paintings, glass ware, swords, helmets, candle-sticks, toilet ornaments and curious jewelry. There were old doors and hinges, keys, plates, spoons, and in fact everything that was used in those days, even down to "stick pins," and needles.

This Museum was originally built for a temple to Mercury, and must have been very handsome. There is no roof now to cover it.

There were some gruesome things, too, a number of bodies, among them a mother and daughter, as it is supposed, as they were found dead together. There was a negro and a poor dog who had been chained and had evidently died in great agony. There was another man who is supposed to have been drunken at the time he died, as his features are calm as if he had been asleep. Another was doubtless a prisoner as there was an iron band around his waist and a chain. These were not the real bodies, but plaster casts made by pouring liquid plaster into the mould that had formed around the bodies of the melted lava and mud that had surrounded them, and that way every feature is preserved exactly. Even the texture of the clothes they wore is shown.

There were many other very interesting things in the Museum but we could not stay there longer. Of course pots and pans are in themselves not so very interesting but when you think of the awful catastrophe that buried these so long ago, and that they are being now slowly and painfully brought

RECENT EXCAVATIONS IN POMPEII.

to light, and that they show us plainer than books how the people lived in those days, why every one is interesting, and if you look at the plainest one of all you begin to think about the unhappy people who once used it.

The next things pointed out were the deep ruts in the pavements which had been worn in the old days by chariot wheels and they looked as if they were done yesterday. There were stepping stones across each street which were arranged so as to allow a chariot to pass between them and yet be near enough for people to step across without wetting their feet.

We passed up what is called the main street, where the sliding doors proved that these had been stores at one time. In front of every store there was a loop hole cut in the curbstone, so that purchasers could hitch their horses.

. We entered the vestibule of one house which was very well preserved. The courtyard opened from the vestibule and there was a small fountain in the center and right near the vestibule was a small, square fountain to carry away the rain water. A bust of the owner of this house was set on a pedestal, at one side, and on the stumps of arms the visitors hung their coats, and put their hats on the head. The house was that of Cornelio Ruffo — the roof was gone, but all the rooms with their walls could be traced. At the rain-water basin were two beautiful carvings, like tables, nearly perfect. It was a large house.

The bed-rooms, kitchen and other apartments all opened around the court, and nearly all of these rooms were in a good state of preservation. Some of the houses, and in fact most of them have been beautifully decorated, by paintings which have been applied directly on the thick plastering, and the colors are rich and as bright to-day as when put on. In many houses there were fine mosaic pictures, and there was a large mural painting representing a battle. One house had a magnificent fire-place made of beautiful stones, each of a different color, that is on one side. The other side matched, so that there were two stones of each color.

We next visited the bakery where the bread was found. Everything remained just as it was in the days of old, except that the bread was in the Museum. There were several great jars where the bread was once mixed and three big mills where the wheat was ground, besides several other objects. The oven had an arched door, and I think is nearly the same as the ovens now used in bakeries. There is no roof to this bakery and at the farther end you see the surface of the earth ten or twelve feet thick above it, with good-sized trees growing.

We next visited the prison and there fastened to the wall with a heavy chain was the shrunken body of a poor man, who unable to escape had died apparently in dreadful agony. There was little left of him but dried up flesh and bones. We left this place with great relief and next saw the plunge bath, which was in a small building very well preserved, and the floor was laid in fine mosaic work.

We also went to see the public baths, which are nearly well enough preserved to use now. These are near the Forum and are very well arranged, very large and beautifully decorated. I do not believe there are any public baths in the world as handsome and large as these. They take up one whole block, over a hundred and fifty feet wide and nearly two hundred feet deep.

There are three divisions, one was for the fire and servants, and the others were for men and women. There was steam, and cold and hot water besides. In the furnace room they found pitch, and at the door of the main entrance they found a box of money and a sword, which the doorkeeper probably left in trying to escape. There are copper boilers between the men and women's compartments, and in the dressing room the pegs burned out and left the holes where the wooden pegs had been to hang clothes on. There are seats here cut out of lava, which it seems must have been handy building material when Pompeii was built. This room had had a glass roof, a passage led into the cold room, which had a bath tub of marble as big as an ordinary room and about three feet deep. There is one large room called the Tepidarium, with a large bronze brazier and a bench or so. The floors are tiled, and the walls were arched and beautifully decorated with high relief stucco figures, and all richly colored. This was a warm but not hot room and was to prepare the bathers for the hot air or steam rooms. The steam room and the hot room are both beautifully decorated and are fairly well preserved, but the women's baths which are smaller are nearly in ruins. The water for these baths came from a reservoir across the street.

It would need but little work or expense to put part of these baths into working order and it is a pity that it is not done for the benefit of the men and women who work in these ruins.

The Forum or public market place was next on the programme. Here, nothing remained but a line of broken columns, and occasionally an altar where sacrifices had been made, and one place was a temple where it was supposed an oracle spoke to the people while it was really a man who did so from a convenient place inside.

We finally came to the lower gate of the city where the most of the bodies had been found. They had tried to get out but the smoke and cinders had suffocated them. There was a small fountain near here in what had evidently been a business street, and the guide called our attention to the places that had been worn away by the hands of the people who had drank at this fountain. The left hand had left the deepest impression.

We mounted a little rise of ground that is undoubtedly the covering of another house, and from there we had a splendid view of the whole city as far as it is laid bare. From here we could see the Gate of Herculaneum with the beautiful tomb beyond, and the ruins of several buildings outside of the walls. Near by was what they call the House of the Musicians and of the Vestals. There are a number of houses built on the sloping rocks where the sea once came, and some of these houses are three stories high. The streets seem nearly all to converge into the Forum, but yet they are laid out in blocks. One house I remember was called the house of the surgeon because many bronze and steel surgical instruments were found there. The Forum is about four or five hundred yards from the Gate of Herculaneum. On the west side the streets run down towards the bay, and all the houses uncovered on those streets are public buildings. It seems that houses had mural paintings that represented the business the owner followed, one is called the house of the hunter, another silversmith, another a dyer's, and so on.

In the Forum place there is an arch and at the opening of another street is another triumphal arch, not so well preserved as the first. There was a milk store or dairy in one house, and one fine one was the school of Gladiators. There is one place called the quarter of theaters. In that are the Temple of Hercules, the Temple of Isis, the Temple of Æsculapius, and the two theaters I mentioned before, and also a large open space enclosed by two porticos. Probably this was the ball ground.

About five or six hundred feet from there in the southeast corner lies the amphitheatre, which presents a fine view, with a fringe of great trees at the top of the eastern side, and with the burning mountain for a background.

There is quite a large space that is not yet excavated that is now covered over with vines and trees and shrubbery. Only about one-eighth of the whole has been excavated, and as far as they could tell they tried to get at the wealthiest people's houses. It was twelve miles around and now six gates and twelve towers have been found. It must have been a beautiful city, though not so very large, and what we have in the way of furniture to show our wealth these ancients put into the durable decorations of their homes which has lasted to show us how they lived in those old days.

The excavations are carried on with great system, men go ahead into each street and dig, and each basketful of dirt or ashes is sifted for valuables and women take the shell-shaped baskets on their heads and walk off with them as stately as a queen with a heavy crown. Often a statue is found, or a bag of coins, or some household implement. Everything that is rescued from the ashes of the past is valuable, and the bosses keep such a close lookout that it has to be a smarter tourist than I to get a chance to buy one.

When one stands on the hill and looks around at the half buried city, and notes the long rows of broken columns and crumbled walls, at the sea shining there and then at Vesuvius so near by, it makes one shudder to think that at any moment a great tidal wave could dash in, or a new convulsion bury the whole in an hour beneath a new weight of lava.

We got our money's worth out of that guide for we went everywhere, into every place we could crawl, and asked him questions until he looked as though he would drop, and as we were getting hungry anyhow, we went back to the little inn for our dinner, which was unmentionable, but we had to eat it or starve.

CHAPTER XII.

VESUVIUS.

DURING our dinner at the little inn we had the satisfaction of hearing some fine music played by some Italians on a mandolin and guitar, and watched the smoke curl majestically up and sail away from the mouth of the grim monster beyond, and as soon as we had finished we got ready to make the ascent of the mountain of fire.

Charles always had bad luck with horses. If there ever was one old nag more decrepit or lazy or vicious than another he somehow chose it; not that he did it on purpose, for he tried his best to get good ones and he certainly paid for the best, but just as soon as we would get well under way the wretched brute would show his tactics, and it was usually too late to turn back, and if he did get another, that too, would do something, from standing still, or lying down to kicking or trying to bite. This time Charles got one that would jump stiff-legged every time he was struck, and if he wasn't struck he wouldn't move at all. But, after much argument on the part of the guide, which was mostly done with a stick, the miserable beast consented to follow my horse about three or four yards behind, which made it unpleasant, for the dust was so light and fine that every time the horse's hoofs struck the ground clouds would rise and bid fair to choke Charles. If it had only been fresh dust I don't think it would have been so bad, but this was the dust of ages, and we both regretted that we didn't wear veils. The road was narrow and the sun was hot and it was altogether a most uncomfortable ride.

After two miles of this we stopped at an inn to give our horses a rest, and it was then that we discovered that a barefooted boy had run with us all the way for the sake of earning a little money holding our horses. He had held on to the tail of Charles's horse the whole way. He grinned so that his white teeth showed through the dust on his face like pearls in an oyster and his black eyes looked so jolly that no one could have refused him. He gave the horses a drink and wiped the dust out of their eyes and noses, and as we had rested for about fifteen minutes and had a cool drink ourselves we were ready to start on.

The ascent began gradually along a plain where two specks were visible, and as we galloped on they grew in size until we saw that one was a monk and the other a boy guide. We soon left them behind and began our ascent through the slippery lava. These rows of lava lay on every side and some were warm, while other places were cold. We kept climbing up and up until we came to a little corral made of pieces of lava, and there we left our horses and started up on foot. A couple of men handed us some ropes to take hold of, but we found it easier to climb without being dragged along and so dismissed them and started like braves on a warpath.

Charles stopped after a while to take the view but the guide and I kept on, thinking that he would overtake us in a few minutes, but somehow he missed the right path and went in a direction that would have taken him to a very dangerous place, if he had kept on. He was for a short time completely lost, and when we found that he did not follow us we decided that it was best to sit down and wait, and we whistled and called, but we were looking down the path by which we had come, when imagine our surprise to see him come slipping and springing over the lava, which was loose in most parts and had not been cleared away to make a path. It was with the greatest difficulty that he reached us, all out of breath.

The lava crust looked like huge misshapen monsters lying huddled asleep. It had flowed on and cooled in waves and billows, and was full of crevices and treacherous spots. As we started up again the ground began to feel hot under our feet, and fumes of sulphur came from the crevices.

A little further on we reached what we thought was the top but it was not and we found there was another hill ahead. Just a little beyond us was a fat man trying to reach the top. He would slip and flounder and every few minutes he would stop to wipe

LAVA FROM VESUVIUS.

his red face, and swear at the guide for making him believe that it was nothing to climb up here. We slipped and grappled with each other and the guide as the loose bits of sulphur and lava slid from under our feet, but at last we reached the summit of the crater, and at the same moment got a puff of sulphur smoke that nearly took our breath away.

When we could see, we found we were on the crest of the rim of the Volcano. Hundreds of feet below us there was an abyss, from which the flames and smoke were coming. I cannot describe that hole. It was such a surprise to me. Charles thought it would look like a Christmas pudding with the steam coming out of the top, but it proved to be entirely different, and was a deep hole with sulphur fumes coming up in great clouds, and once in a while a burst of smoke and ashes and stones.

We struggled around, away over to the far side, where the fumes nearly choked us. We wedged some great stones loose and sent them rolling down into the crater, and as they went they dislodged and carried hundreds of smaller ones along, all bouncing up and down and leaving a cloud of dust behind. I had to laugh to see these little ones go following the big one along, like the New York gamins after a gorgeous drum major.

We went around to the other side where were great fissures in the rocks and steam and sulphur smoke were coming out in volumes, and there was another vein in which hot lava was coursing and it sounded like running water.

In another place we put our hands over a little hole to see if it was hot. It was. The ground under us was in constant commotion and trembled and rumbled, and all over were crevices and fissures emitting fumes and steam, and we could plainly hear the roar of burning lava. In the old crater down below, the lava was red hot and flowing down slowly.

We returned to the other side, where there was a small party gathered together, and one of the old guides was trying to loosen a monstrous stone from its bed and send it down the crater. He was doing this at the risk of his own life, for if the earth under him gave way, and he was standing on a small projection of rock, he would have been dashed to pieces on the rocks below.

At last he got it loose and the rock began to slide. He had barely time to jump up and grasp the hand of another guide before the whole piece he was standing on began to slide and went down with a roar. The stone struck another projection of rock and flew into a thousand pieces, which were swallowed in the dark mouth of the crater.

The guide then went around with his hat for the people to give him something which we all did willingly, except the fat man who reluctantly gave him five centimes (one penny), and that caused the guide to give him such a look of unspeakable disgust that we all laughed.

After that we amused ourselves by picking up curious bits of sulphur and lava, and examining fissures to find out if they were hot by holding our hands over them, until we were quite satisfied that they were.

Once there was an awful roar and rumble and smoke belched forth in great force and frightened all of us, but the guides say that was nothing unusual, and that often the sides of the crater get red hot and stones are thrown great distances through the air and roll down the mountain side where they gather in heaps.

One feels creepy when standing on the

top of that crater, and hears the lava simmering under him, and feels the heat and listens to the hollow sound which comes from some of the fissures. The guides told us that after every new eruption the shape of the crater changes, and that makes it very dangerous. It is only recently that the Volcano has been photographed and on returning to Naples I got several very fine photographs of this wonderful mountain.

It is curious but I have not found anyone who ever noticed the surrounding scenery when making the ascent or descent of Vesuvius, and I suppose this is because it needs all one's faculties to keep from slipping until one gets to the top and then no one can think of anything but this outlet of internal fires. These fires are liable to break out again at any hour, and be just as destructive as before, and no one can tell which side the lava will run out from.

Naples itself is said to be built over two extinct volcanos, and if we can judge by the Grotto de Cannes it is so, and they are not dead but only asleep. Let us hope they will never awake.

As it was now nearly sundown we started back to Naples. For a little way it was not easy traveling as the stones and sulphur slipped, and that way it was nearly impossible to keep one's feet, but when we reached a place where there was a thin layer of ashes we fairly slid down like rockets. We could not stop until we reached a level place covered with ashes, but a little relieved to feel that we were safe and unhurt. We were completely out of breath when we reached a level landing, and sat down to rest.

Here the guide called our attention to the view, and it was indeed beautiful. The whole bay was in plain sight with its thirty miles of coast spread out before us.

There lay Naples in the distance, the windows gleaming in the sun's last rays, Sorrento and Castlemarre and dozens of small towns were in plain sight, and the lovely island of Capri made a grand showing in the late shadows of sunset. The white roads running along the coast or leading towards the interior were plainly visible and the ruins of Pompeii were almost at our feet. It was a sight never to be forgotten.

The guide and I started on alone again, leaving Charles to sit on a lump of lava and ponder. Charles is one of those whose souls are full of admiration for the beauties of Nature, and it seemed as if he could never bear to tear himself away from a position where he had a noble view like this. He would appear to be in a happy sort of trance and it was always with difficulty that he could tear his eyes away from it, and bring his mind back to the everyday things. A nobler, more high-minded, and lovable man I never met, and while we were together I learned to feel a friendship for him that I am sure will last forever. Perhaps I am not old enough to feel so deeply, but I think I cared all the more for him seeing how completely he would become lost to everything but the beauty and grandeur of the things we saw.

The guide and I took arms and went downward again, slipping, struggling, and sliding, and always at the risk of rolling completely over, and when we reached another comparatively level space we sat down and shouted to Charles to come, or it would be dark. He roused and started; but, as it needs two or more together, to support and sustain each other, he slipped and floundered and tumbled along in such a fashion that he looked to be all arms and legs. I was thankful that no one was about with a camera when I came down, as I am noted for the length of my own legs and arms, as they are long and not broad. It must have been funny. Charles soon reached us and we mounted on our prancing steeds, which were more willing to go down than they had been to come up. They picked their way carefully over the loose stones and lava, and I expected every minute to go headlong, but we at last reached a line of smoother ground covered with ashes, and then it was not so bad. We could see little specks below which proved to be people on horseback when we drew near.

On our route we passed a place where men were at work making preparations for the Emperor of Germany, who was to visit the mountain in a few days. They were building a booth and fixing it up for a special dining room, I think.

We stopped at the inn only long enough

to change our horses for the carriage which was waiting, and asked for water. This was brought, and just as we were going to drink I noticed several specks, and as I looked closer I found it was full of little white insects, and goodness knows what else, and they were swimming around at a lively rate. I handed the glass back and so did Charles, saying that we had asked for drinking water, not an aquarium. How many we had drank in the morning in our pink lemonade I do not know. The men looked surprised when we handed back the water and told us that it was fine water, that it was perfectly pure and good. Maybe it was, but we liked our fishes cooked.

When we returned to Naples that evening dinner was about half over, but we did justice to the remainder. There were a number of men there who were full of fun, and they were singing the donkey song, in which one sings the song and all the rest join in the chorus braying like donkeys. It was very funny, at first, but they kept it up until nearly morning. We were very tired, but it seemed as if my mind was so full of the wonderful sights we had crowded into one day that I could never sleep again. If I did drop off for a moment I would wake with a start thinking I was falling into the great red crater, or that ashes and burning lava were pursuing me among the ruins of Pompeii; but I was and always shall be glad that I had seen those two great sights. It is one thing to go through even the greatest edifices and see the most wonderful things men ever did, and quite another to see the power of God, as shown at Pompeii and Vesuvius.

CHAPTER XIII.

NAPLES AND CAPRI.

THE morning following our visit to Pompeii and Vesuvius we felt tired and lame, but every time we lifted our eyes to the smoking peak we were thankful that we had been up there.

We went to see the Aquarium which is well worth seeing. It has a very fine collection of fish of almost every known species, among them some cuttle-fish. The keeper tied a poor little crab on a string and let it down into the tank near one of them. There was a rush and a twining of long arms and the crab was gone. The octopus creep along so smoothly that you can hardly see them move, their long arms reaching out in all directions for prey. Their eyes are cold and evil, and it makes one shudder to see them. There were a number of squids in one tank, and it had been a habit to poke sticks at them to see them emit the inky fluid, but it seems that the Emperor had requested that that should not be done any more as he thought it cruel, and we did not see the performance.

It would take a book full to describe all the curious fish and other wonders of the deep in this Aquarium. It is said to be the most complete in the world and I do not doubt it. I have always been an eager lover of natural history and I could hardly tear myself away, but we had many other things to see.

We went from there to the National Museum where there was a large collection of things from Pompeii, but they were nearly all of the same class as those shown in the museum at Pompeii: such as lamps, candlesticks, vases and plaster casts. There was one fine piece of mosaic, representing a ferocious dog chained, and with the words *Cave canem* also in mosaic.

There were also many pieces of old armor and arms, and relics of various kinds, such as you will see in almost any museum, but the things that most interested me were those from Pompeii.

After we had seen all that was in the museum we went and made a few purchases, chiefly photographs, and walked around to see the different parts of the city, which we found very interesting, particularly the older part, and where the poor live.

We often hear how hard the poor foreigners have to work and how little they are paid. I know they are not paid much, but I didn't see anybody working as the people do in America. Here it was a lazy sort of movement with much lounging and many rests. If anyone in Naples worked as hard and continually as they do in New York, such a person would surely get rich in a short time even at the pay offered at Naples, for living is so very cheap for those who are content with poverty. Macaroni with a sauce of tomatoes and fried onions forms the chief of their diet, with once in a while a little fish or fruit, and that doesn't cost much.

On our return to the hotel we made plans to go to Capri, and then take a boat to Sorrento, and drive from there to Castlemarre. We retired early and rested well, and were up early to start. We took the boat which crosses the bay to Capri, and were about an hour and a half crossing, and it was a delightful trip.

There were men who sang all the way to stringed instruments, and they knew only three songs, and these they repeated over and over until I learned them by heart. They were Finaculi-Finacula, Belle Napoli, and Marguerite; not the Marguerite sung here, but one much sweeter I think.

Capri seen from a distance looks like a great barren rock, but as you approach it shows greener and fresher, and when close to it you find that it is wonderfully fertile. We landed in a small cove, which swarmed with small boats whose owners seemed to exist for the sole purpose of taking travelers to see the blue grotto. We were soon on the way to this famous place, and ducked our heads obediently, to raise them again at the word of command after having traversed the low entrance. We raised our eyes to find ourselves in fairyland, and the farther you go the more beautiful it is.

From some cause or other the light reflects from the water on the rocks above and gives them a rich, deep blue tint, that is light or dark as the shadows fall. The effect was as if the whole cave was made of one big broken sapphire. The oars as they dipped in the water looked like bright silver, and a little boy plunged in the water to swim and looked like a silver image come to life. We were not allowed to remain long here as the steamer was ready to go, and so we regretfully left this beautiful blue wonder, and hastened on board, and were soon on the way to the town of Capri, near the middle of the island.

About dinner-time we landed at Capri and went to the hotel for dinner, and it was there I first tasted nespoli, a delicious fruit something like a plum, but with three or four large seeds and a thick skin. I think it would be a success if introduced into this country.

I won't dwell upon that dinner but the

drive we took after was worth mention. We took a carriage and went up to the top of the island which is like a promontory and is covered everywhere with vines and fruits. There are steps cut in the rock up which the people toil, the women with baskets of fish or other things on their heads. They take those long stairs as though it was nothing, and did not act as though they felt the climb.

The view from this high point is enchanting. The City of Naples and curve of the bay is seen from a new point, and show new beauties everywhere, and Old Vesuvius stands with a new outline but always interesting.

We drove over to Anti-Capri, and turned around and went to a small village on the other side. What a queer, quaint little place it was! The houses were mostly low and poor, but the luxuriance of the trees and flowers, fruit and vines made up for any lack, and it looked calm and peaceful here. I wondered what these people would do if a string of boys and men were to file down one of their funny little streets shouting, "Huxtra! Huxtra! all about the great railway disaster!" Charles went down one street to make some purchases, and I bought some nespoli of a girl. I told her as best I could, but she gave me twice as much as I had asked for, about two cents' worth, and I gave her the money and walked off regardless of her blank face. I felt happy to think that I had for once got the best of a bargain, with an Italian.

Our time was short as the boat for Sorrento was about to start, and we scrambled down to the landing with considerable difficulty. From where we had been we could see Capri below us, the steamer and all that was going on down there, and a busy scene it was. We caught the boat, and soon Capri became a rock again, this time behind us, and Sorrento lay before. We were taken ashore by small boats, and when we landed we engaged a carriage to take us to Castlemarre, but we found we would have to walk to the top of the hill to get it, and that hill was a long one, but we reached the top at last and were soon comfortably seated in a small carriage drawn by two horses.

As we drove through the streets of Sorrento we found that we were objects of curiosity, particularly to the ladies who were seated in the balconies. The most of these ladies were very handsome with large dark eyes and hair.

The roads further on were lined with orange and lemon trees, and we hailed a small boy who had his arms full and bought all he had for fifty centimes (ten cents), and they were fresh and tasted good, as we were thirsty and the road dusty and the day hot.

The road wound in and out, between farms, gardens, and trees, and crossed deep ravines where we could look down and see boats moving to and fro, and at times catch glimpses of the ever beautiful bay, or of Vesuvius, which always seemed to step into the landscape from whatever point with its charm of terribleness. Sometimes we saw the smoking point from between trees, sometimes from between houses, over rocks or from the water, or across it — always the same and always changing. I hope I may never forget the pictures I have seen of that volcano as long as I may live. Some of these little glimpses seen through intervening trees were worth a hundred trips to Europe; but I couldn't help wishing that there might be a little eruption that wouldn't hurt anything, that I might see at a safe distance before I left.

We reached Castlemarre which is a pretty city, as also is Sorrento, but we had not time for a very long study of its beauties as we had to take the train back to Naples.

The train started and we were soon moving through the little fishing villages along the coast, where the men were building boats or mending nets. The streets were so narrow that it was impossible to see down through them. We brought the rest of the oranges that we had bought, and at every station there was a crowd of beggars, all crying out that they were hungry. Just as we were pulling out of one station I threw an orange to one fellow who was wailing out his woes loudly, and it hit him directly in the mouth and hit him hard, though I did not intend to hurt him. I was glad the train was moving.

It was not long before we reached Naples and we brought splendid appetites along. When I entered my room at the hotel a most

surprising sight met my gaze, for there all over my floor was a perfect billow of white lace. I could not imagine where it came from, until I saw Selim, the dog, all curled up on the remains of the lace window curtain. As soon as he saw that I was mad he looked up at me with such a droll and guilty expression that I had to laugh instead of whipping him as he deserved.

I gathered up the pieces and twisted the curtain up so that the torn places were not so noticeable, and during it all he watched me with the keenest interest, thinking, I suppose, that he would pull it all down and chew it up again if I went off another time and left him all day alone.

The next morning we took a cab and soon stood upon the platform of the railway station. It was all decked with flags and rich curtains and other things to make it look attractive, as the Emperor of Germany was to arrive soon. We had our tickets for Rome and on the way passed the train bearing the Emperor of Germany. All of the stations along the route were decked with flags and flowers, and crowds of people were waiting his arrival. Soon we were out of sight of Naples and had caught our last glimpse of Vesuvius and were looking forward to Rome.

CHAPTER XIV.

ROME.

WE arrived at Rome about three o'clock that afternoon, after a very pleasant ride through a country made familiar by much study of geography and history at home and of the guide-book abroad.

As soon as we arrived we went to a hotel and after a good wash and dinner we started out to see the sights, and drove to the principal places. We left the Piazza Spagna and drove along the Corso, which is the principal street and on to the Piazza Venezia, and past the old Forum Trajano, and down the Via Bonello to the Forum Romanum, past the famous Colosseum and then around to the principal churches, and after that up to the Capitoline Hill, and back to the hotel. This ride took up all the afternoon and we thought we had done very well for so short a time, as we had got the plan of the great city and all its wonders fixed in our minds. The next morning we started early and went back to the Colosseum, which is indeed a great sight. The enormous size of the place and the remembrance of what it was for made it doubly interesting. There are four stories or tiers on one side, the outer portion of which is in good preservation. The other side seems to have been partly demolished and carried away. All around it are great fragments of stone, broken columns, and crumbled walls of other buildings now forgotten. The Arch of Titus stands at one side, and that of Constantine near by, both of them showing what the pomps and vanities of this world come to.

We mounted the great stone steps inside the Colosseum and soon were at the top and looking down on the great Arena. The tiers upon tiers of seats once filled with shouting people now serve for nesting places for flocks of little birds, and all over the walls are holes worn in by the elements, though our guide declared it was caused by the people taking the iron out for balls, at one time in the history of Rome. But the holes are there, so many that it is fairly honeycombed. The floor of the Colosseum or Arena has been partially uncovered so that one may see the dungeons below where the wild beasts were kept, and also places where the unfortunate prisoners were confined until it pleased those in power to get up a celebration and bring them out to be torn to pieces in the Arena. Down in that excavation the cells were built in regular streets with thick walls to the dungeons.

No escape was possible. The whole of the place has not been excavated, and that part left to show the form of the old Arena is smooth, and railed off so no one can fall down into the pits. All around the Arena and below the first tier of seats there were small rooms which doubtless held animals, as they are strong and massive. Nature has been kinder to the Amphitheatre at Pompeii than to the Colosseum in Rome.

Just outside of this great place we stopped to admire the surroundings, which are of the greatest interest. The massive Arch of Constantine is a work of art, covered as it is with carving in relief relating to his exploits. The Arch of Titus is not so highly ornamented but it has several points where there are fine carved figures in high relief. They relate to his achievements, and represent, I think, triumphal processions, and there is an inscription showing the date and for whom it was erected.

Near by the Colosseum are the crumbling remains of the Gladiators' Fountain, where they used to stop for good luck and wash before going to fight. There is a conical stone pillar from which the water flowed, and the remains of the circular basin.

After having examined the Colosseum from one end to the other and viewed these two arches from every side, we went to the Roman Forum or rather the place where it was once. I would like to tell all about this Forum, what it was for and who had stood here in time long past, but I refrain, for I suppose it would be telling people what they knew long ago, and I suppose the most of those who have not been there have seen pictures of what it looks like now, but it was very new to me. There are a few columns still standing, but the most of those that once enclosed this vast court are gone. There is one large fluted column set upon a stone foundation which was doubtless some sort of monument. In every direction there are fragments which show what this place must have been "in the brave days of old." It is surrounded by fine buildings, and within the enclosure s'ands the triumphal arch of Septimus Severus, the old fellow that thought he ought to get twenty-five hours' work out of each twenty-four, and had himself kept awake by a gong. This arch is very handsome and is richly carved, but is not nearly as well preserved as that of Constantine, which shows scarcely any signs of decay. At the base of the Septimus Severus Arch are some fine carvings in relief. This arch is seventy-five feet high and will last for several generations more. The pavement of the old Forum is almost entire. Charles got up on the stump of one column and I on another and we spouted Julius Cæsar at each other, and felt that we were old Roman orators. Nothing remains of the former greatness of the old Forum except a pile of ruins covered by earth and beautiful poppies, and of the splendid Temple of Saturn there remain but a few columns.

There was a regular line of forums laid out — first coming the Forum of Vespasian, next the Forum of Minerva, with a temple to Minerva at the end, the Forum of Augustus, then the Forum of Cæsar, opposite this, and having the Temple of Venus set in the centre, then came the Forum of Trajan. The Forum Romanum was built in a sort of cornering way from the others, nearly at the foot of the hill where is the Basilica Julia. On one side are the remains of a rostrum, and near that the Arch of Augustus, and a temple to Vesta. There are other ruins of massive buildings, most of them of great beauty. There is a large square building, or rather its remains, called the *Atrium Vestæ*, just beyond the round temple. The Forum Romanum is on ground a little below the roadway that is built all around it, and one gets a very good view of it by driving around the whole. I do not know what it is that makes ruins so interesting, but I think that I could stay forever wandering around among the old moss-grown and rain-beaten stones without wanting or caring to know anything about their history.

The Forum of Trajan is a bit of the old world surrounded by the new. It is on sunken ground, several feet below the sidewalk, and there is an iron fence with stone posts all around it. Inside the enclosure are many broken columns, not one entire. These temples and forums have been covered with earth and are now excavated. It is thought that only a small portion of this

THE RUINS OF THE FORUM, ROME.

Forum has been brought to light. Trajan's column stands in the centre of the farthest end from the entrance. This column is a wonder, and has carvings in a spiral pattern three feet wide, winding from the bottom to the top. It is said to represent pictures of the war with the Dacians, and it has one continuous procession of men and animals. The column is hollow and has steps inside. It once had Trajan's statue on top, now it has some saint. This column is 147 feet high, and it is said that the old emperor is buried beneath the base of the column. I wonder some one does not try to dig him out, to put in a museum. There are two churches behind the plaza or open space back of this Forum.

After we had wandered over all these places we went to the Basilica Julia, which is almost all crumbled away, having very little to show except ruined arches overgrown with shrubs and poppies. Under the eastern end of this immense building can be seen the remains of the main conduit of the Cloaca Maxima, which was built to drain the water off the marshes.

Modern streets, some of them very busy ones, have been cut right through these ruins, and that way it has been hard to preserve things that ought to be the nation's pride. Just to the east stand the ruins of the Temple of Castor and Pollux. Across the Via Sacra is a temple to Romulus, and near the Via Miranda is the rest of one to Antonine and Faustine. In fact there are more temples and arches and forums than I could describe separately. There is a large tract of ground thickly covered with the remains of what was the centre of Rome in those days.

The Basilica Constantini stands on another side from that of the Basilica Julia. Seen from the side of the Via Sacra (or Holy Way) it shows an imposing front of three great arches flanked by small ones, at the side, and with others as a sort of foundation. The inner parts of these great arches form immense rooms, richly decorated on the sides and overhead. These are covered with what was evidently the roof. There was a large platform in front, and evidences that it extended much farther than it does now. Charles and I climbed up on two great stone abutments still better to admire this stupendous building. Near the Basilica de Constantine are the ruins of the palace of Cæsar, rising in tiers and losing themselves under the trees that have grown in the earth that has covered this palace completely. The whole place looks from a distance much like the ruins of the house of blocks a child builds, but it is immense. There are arches everywhere and in some places the outlines of rooms show that the floors have been inlaid with various marbles in mosaic work. On one of the lower terraces there are many statues standing against a wall, which have probably fallen from different portions of the palace, and all been brought here. In all I counted six terraces or stories, and this, I think, must have been a fine palace in its day.

We had started up the steps that led to the Capitoline Hill, and from there we had a fine view of all the parts of the city that most interested us, and made a long turn and went up a road that we supposed would take us to the palace of the Cæsars, but we took a wrong road and went half a mile only to return again and climb up to the entrance, where we saw a notice that it was all free, but the guides that sprung up from behind every stone, it seemed, were willing to accept what we were willing to give. And it was worth all we paid and more to see those odd old household utensils and curious crockery and many other relics found in the work of excavation. There were remains of fine balconies and mosaic work, and mural paintings. In one place the guides pointed out a portion of a wall said to have been built by Romulus and Remus. It was made of huge blocks of stone without cement. I often think of the way they boomed that town up and got other people to come in with them and take corner lots without advertising, and I think they were smarter than men are nowadays.

The Capitoline Hill as it is now does not show so very many signs of what it once was, still the Museum that holds all the rich bronzes that have been dug out of the ruins, the statuary and carvings of different kinds and other relics is a place one could spend years in. The ancient buildings have been altered by different persons so that though it is beautiful now on the Capitoline Hill it is not so interesting as it might have been had they left the old edifices alone. Steps now lead up to the buildings flanked by large statues of Castor and Pollux with horses, and directly at the top of the steps is a statue of Marcus Aurelius on horseback. The house of the Senators has been rebuilt.

On this hill there are many curious relics, among them being some of the milestones of the Appian Way. It would be simply impossible to describe them all, but they are wonderful. There are busts or bas-reliefs of all the rulers of ancient Rome and numbers of other people, besides gods and goddesses. It was here that the original statue of the Dying Gladiator was found. A woman guide shows you the Tarpian Rock, where people were hurled down to death. From the Capitoline Hill one gets a fine view of all the ruins, particularly the Forum Romanum, and there is a flight of steps which leads up from there by way of the Temple of Vespasian.

The Palatine Hill is on the south side of the Forum, and it had a number of temples to Jove, Apollo and other gods, and several royal residences. This hill was joined to another smaller one by great buildings on deep foundations. The ruins are scattered over a large space and have among them the ancient palaces of Caligula, Augustus, Septimus Severus and others. There were temples everywhere, baths and one dwelling supposed to have been that of Flavia. There was also what remains of the palace of Tiberius, and the guide said that it was on this hill that Romulus and Remus had lived and they show a cave for the wolf. The guide who did not show that cave would not be doing his duty.

We went out the Appian Way, and here were much struck by the magnitude of the ancient works. The Appian Way starts from the Arch of Constantine, and one passes many interesting places. The road outside the city starts from the Capuan gate. About three-quarters of a mile from the Arch of Constantine are the baths of Caracalla. These would have accommodated 1600 bathers at once and the ruins are most interesting, consisting mostly of immense arches, broken columns, mural paintings, mosaic floors and sculptured stones like tables, besides deep basins in the floor which is perfect in some places. There were many famous statues taken from this place. There are many places along the Appian Way where the old pavement still lies, and on each side are ruins of tombs, temples, baths, and fountains, all overgrown with weeds and vines and sometimes trees. There is a great aqueduct, that of Claudius I believe, which is massive and still a marvel of the skill of the old Romans. Part of the Appian Way is called the old road and part is called the new road; this last is macadamized. Some of the ruins were very interesting, but we could not stop to examine them all as we would have liked to do.

One of the gates, that of St. Sebastian, which is one of the outlets to the Appian Way, shows the ruined Arch of Drusus. There were tombs of various kinds to be seen near by, but we had so little time that we could not stop for more than a general view.

We went to the wonderful Pantheon, which was originally built for the burial-place of Agrippa, now it is used to bury many prominent persons. I think Michael Angelo is buried there. The dome, and indeed the whole place, is grand and beautiful, but sombre somehow. Just behind the Pantheon is another circular building which is called the baths of Agrippa. When we went to the Pantheon we had to wait until about 200 Italian soldiers had gone around. They did not seem to take up hardly any space in that great room.

We went to St. Peter's, which joins the Vatican. No words of mine or anybody else can worthily describe this great church. Charles was overcome by the grandeur and sat lost in admiration while I went up to the dome and from there I mounted to the gilt ball on top. This looks about as big as an apple from the ground, but it will hold about sixteen people. I don't think any person living could tell all the beauties of Rome's great buildings. It takes one's breath away. It is almost as grand as mountains and the ocean.

While in Rome we visited all the great churches, and found them all interesting from various causes, though of course none could compare with St. Peter's. We saw the

"Scala Santa" where worshippers go up the long flight of steps on their knees. We saw all those wonderful statues and paintings that make of Rome one vast museum. In fact, I think we saw all the sights travelers are bound and obliged to take in. Some day I hope to go back to Rome and study each of the wonders in detail, though what I have seen will live in my mind forever.

I forgot to mention that some of the most beautiful views of the great city are those which take in glimpses of the Tiber. One in particular shows the tower of St. Angelo across the river, and on the bridge are ten or twelve statues of heroic size. This tower is of great historic interest, and was the key to the city. The bridge was closed for some reason and we could not go to the tower. There are so many public and private works of art both ancient and modern in Rome that anyone would be confused trying to remember them. The plazas are like museums with their magnificent statues and fountains. There stands before the Pantheon an obelisk on a beautiful pedestal, and there is another great triumphal column with thousands of carved figures upon it on the Piazza Colonna, called Colonna Antonina. There is another larger obelisk on the Piazza del Popolo. On the Palatine Hill, the ruins of the Palace of Caligula are massive and grand, and everywhere is seen the great arch which is the fundament of nearly all the ruined architecture of Rome.

Our visit to the catacombs of St. Calisto was one that I shall never forget. The entrance is through a small building on the Appian Way, about three-quarters of a mile from the city. We were conducted by three Trappist monks who act as guides. They are allowed to talk. The rest of the brother-

THE APPIAN WAY, ROME.

hood are vowed to silence. There are other catacombs, but these are the largest and in the best condition. There were about twenty persons, among them some steamer friends, waiting to go down and Charles and I joined the party. We went down two flights of stairs and through long, winding passages that seem endless, and indeed it is said that the catacombs of Rome if placed in a line would measure about 545 miles, but they wind in and out and sometimes there are four or five tiers or stories and one might wander, if lost, for days before finding an outlet. The passageways are about four feet wide, sometimes less, and on each side in crevices and niches are bodies and bones, and occasionally a lamp. Generally there is a slab or piece of stone with a name on it, and in some places it is hollowed out in large vaults, for families apparently. On several of the walls of these larger places are mural paintings of saints, and in these places are shelves where coffins could be deposited, and other places are arched for the reception of statues and sarcophagi. There is a chapel where on St. Cecelia's day mass is celebrated. Among the notables buried in this place were several popes, two of them still there but the others have been taken away. The dead bones here are not ranged into such fanciful shapes as in the Capuchins but the sight of so many miles of passages lined on all sides by the forgotten dead, and the knowledge that in tier on tier above were the same depressing sights, it is no wonder that I felt very small and little and was very glad to get out into the sunlight again, even if the way was lined with tombs. One was a great tower-like structure, and was the tomb of Cecelia Matella whoever she was. It has withstood the ravages of time better than the rest of them.

We went to the catacombs of the Capuchin monks where the skulls and bones of the dead are arranged in a manner that would seem ingenious and pretty, if it were not that all the fanciful arrangements of arches, flowers, vases, etc., were made of different bones of the bodies gathered there. There is one place where there is holy soil from Calvary, and the bodies are buried in this for fifty years, and are then taken out and used to decorate some other niche. These poor bones and skulls are polished up nicely before they are put in. It is horrible and seems as if it is not right to mix the bones up so that nobody could ever find his own.

Seeing so much of the past almost made me believe that all Rome was dead, but it is not; it is very much alive, and there are so many foreigners there that it has a special interest. But, we concerned ourselves more with old Rome than with the new, though of course, we made the most of our time seeing all we could of all parts of the city.

Before I left home I had had a little correspondence with His Eminence, the Cardinal Ledochowski, the Chief of the Propaganda, and I was anxious to see him, as he had written to me inviting me to call on him if ever I went to Rome. I sent in my card, and he remembered instantly all about it, and sent his secretary to ask me to wait a few moments. Then the secretary conducted me to the Cardinal's private room, outside of which were already some twenty persons waiting for a conference, but His Eminence came forward with outstretched hands and said: "And how are you, my dear Tello." This took away my fear of intruding, and I felt more at ease, and we chatted about half an hour, as though we were old friends. Then wishing me the best of luck, he gave me his autograph photograph. I could not see the Pope, as he was too fatigued, having received so many pilgrims the week before. If I could have stayed a few days longer I might have had an interview with him, but unfortunately our time was up.

Cardinal Ledochowski is a stately and noble looking man, with great dignity and power of carriage, but with that he is as gentle as a women. His manner is perfection, and it is an example for all great men. I shall always be glad I met him.

Everyone has read of the wonders of the Vatican. It is like Aladdin's palace. There are galleries on galleries, chapels, museums, libraries, halls and other rooms until the mind is lost in surprise. The royal stairway is most beautiful, with its double line of columns, each higher than the other, and its sculptured archway. There is a long corridor filled with sculpture of every kind and with pictures in the arches opposite the windows. The library is most wonderful. It is paved with marble, and everywhere stand priceless vases and other works of art. There are desks and on every side are paintings, each one a gem. The ceiling is like nothing else. It is covered with paintings and they are done so as to leave a dazzled effect on the mind. Another long gallery in the museum of the Vatican has a line of busts of famous men the whole length, between the windows. The ceiling to this gallery is wonderful with its carvings and pictures. It is the geographical gallery. The Sistine chapel with its lovely statues is also here. The whole of the upper part of the walls, and one end and the ceiling are covered with religious paintings by old masters. The whole place is to my mind the most wonderful building in the world if I can judge by the little I have seen and what

I have read. The gardens around it are worthy of the Vatican, which is large enough to quarter a big army.

One day while I was walking along I saw the King of Italy. Two little boys bowed to him, and he returned their salute. I took courage and raised my hat and bowed, whereupon he did the same. I thought him a fine looking man, but showing the cares and worries of State. I had had an open letter to all American ministers sent me from Mr. Gresham, our Secretary of State, through the kind offices of a good friend, which would probably have gained me an interview with all the Royalty wherever I passed, but by changing our itinerary the letter missed me and wandered all through Spain and Italy and finally reached me a few days before we started for home, too late for its purpose, but not too late for me to thank all those who took so much trouble, particularly during the two or three days after President Cleveland's inauguration.

Charles and I made several other trips about Rome, visiting the Quirinal and all other places of interest mentioned by the guides, but no ten books could tell all we saw. We went to the Trevi fountain where the people say the water is enchanted so that whoever drinks it is obliged to revisit Rome. We drank and threw in a handful of copper money. Selim thought water was good, and started after a drink or to recover our soldi, and he nearly fell in the fountain, which is large and deep, and he looked perfectly discouraged when I scolded him, as much as to say, " what's the use of a fellow trying to make himself useful, and be abused for it?"

We were not traveling for social pleasures, nor any kind of gayety, and so confined ourselves strictly to the business of seeing all we could of every place we visited and as we had done all that could be compassed into those few days, we started back to Florence, where we arrived and were rejoiced to find Aunt Mary quite recovered.

A few days later we started back to Genoa, and remained waiting several days for the *Fulda* to sail. What we saw in Genoa I told in another chapter. At last the *Fulda* was ready to start and so were we. I admit I was homesick, besides I wanted to show my dog to my friends in New York, and I wanted many things, chief of which was to see my parents, and it seemed that the steamer was awfully slow. I was not seasick on this trip. The *Fulda* is an easy steamer anyhow, but I wanted to see New York.

There was a rather more sociable lot of passengers on this steamer than there had been on the *Kaiser Wilhelm*. Among them were Lord and Lady McPherson, who were very friendly to me, and an Italian member of Parliament, and we also grew to be good friends; but Selim furnished about all the diversion there was.

The *Fulda* reached her dock at last, on time, and even sooner than she had been expected, and I said good-bye to Charles who started westward to his home, and to the dear lady who had taken me under her gentle wing, and allowed a lonely boy to call her Aunt Mary during the voyage.

Then I came safely through the Custom House, took a cab and hurried home to find my blessed father and mother busily planning about going to meet me the next morning; were we glad to see each other? I think so. And Selim, he adopted mamma at once and pre-empted her lap as his bed, and promptly went to sleep with a sigh of supreme content, and papa and mamma and I hugged and kissed each other a hundred times. I was glad to get home though I had enjoyed my trip with keen relish. I wish I could feel sure that those who read this little book will enjoy as well as I did my trip to Europe and back.

www.ingramcontent.com/pod-product-compliance
Lightning Source LLC
Chambersburg PA
CBHW032134230426
43672CB00011B/2331